Praise

"What C-Level executives read t... ...make pivotal business decisions. Timeless classics for indispensable knowledge." - Richard Costello, Manager-Corporate Marketing Communication, General Electric (NYSE: GE)

"Want to know what the real leaders are thinking about now? It's in here." - Carl Ledbetter, SVP & CTO, Novell, Inc.

"Priceless wisdom from experts at applying technology in support of business objectives." - Frank Campagnoni, CTO, GE Global Exchange Services

"Unique insights into the way the experts think and the lessons they've learned from experience." - MT Rainey, Co-CEO, Young & Rubicam/Rainey Kelly Campbell Roalfe

"Unlike any other business book." - Bruce Keller, Partner, Debevoise & Plimpton

"The Inside the Minds series is a valuable probe into the thought, perspectives, and techniques of accomplished professionals. By taking a 50,000 foot view, the authors place their endeavors in a context rarely gleaned from text books or treatise." - Chuck Birenbaum, Partner, Thelen Reid & Priest

"A must read for anyone in the industry." - Dr. Chuck Lucier, Chief Growth Officer, Booz-Allen & Hamilton

"A must read for those who manage at the intersection of business and technology." - Frank Roney, General Manager, IBM

"A great way to see across the changing marketing landscape at a time of significant innovation." - David Kenny, Chairman & CEO, Digitas

"An incredible resource of information to help you develop outside-the-box..." - Rich Jernstedt, CEO, Golin/Harris International

"A snapshot of everything you need..." - Charles Koob, Co-Head of Litigation Department, Simpson Thacher & Bartlet

www.Aspatore.com

Aspatore Books is the largest and most exclusive publisher of C-Level executives (CEO, CFO, CTO, CMO, Partner) from the world's most respected companies and law firms. Aspatore annually publishes a select group of C-Level executives from the Global 1,000, top 250 law firms (Partners and Chairs), and other leading companies of all sizes. C-Level Business Intelligence™, as conceptualized and developed by Aspatore Books, provides professionals of all levels with proven business intelligence from industry insiders – direct and unfiltered insight from those who know it best – as opposed to third-party accounts offered by unknown authors and analysts. Aspatore Books is committed to publishing an innovative line of business and legal books, those which lay forth principles and offer insights that when employed, can have a direct financial impact on the reader's business objectives, whatever they may be. In essence, Aspatore publishes critical tools – need-to-read as opposed to nice-to-read books – for all business professionals.

Inside the Minds

The critically acclaimed *Inside the Minds* series provides readers of all levels with proven business intelligence from C-Level executives (CEO, CFO, CTO, CMO, Partner) from the world's most respected companies. Each chapter is comparable to a white paper or essay and is a future-oriented look at where an industry/profession/topic is heading and the most important issues for future success. Each author has been carefully chosen through an exhaustive selection process by the *Inside the Minds* editorial board to write a chapter for this book. *Inside the Minds* was conceived in order to give readers actual insights into the leading minds of business executives worldwide. Because so few books or other publications are actually written by executives in industry, *Inside the Minds* presents an unprecedented look at various industries and professions never before available.

Inside the Minds:
The Food and Beverage Industry

*Industry Leaders on Manufacturing, Marketing, and
Distributing the Edible Goods that Sell*

ASPATORE
BOOKS

Published by Aspatore, Inc.

For corrections, company/title updates, comments or any other inquiries please email info@aspatore.com.

First Printing, 2004
10 9 8 7 6 5 4 3 2 1

ISBN 1-58762-279-3 Library of Congress Control Number: 2004107547

Inside the Minds Managing Editor, Laura Kearns, Edited by Michaela Falls, Proofread by Eddie Fournier, Cover design by Scott Rattray and Ian Mazie

Material in this book is for educational purposes only. This book is sold with the understanding that neither the authors nor the publisher are engaged in rendering medical, legal, accounting, investment, or any other professional service. For legal advice, please consult your personal lawyer.

This book is printed on acid free paper.

A special thanks to all the individuals who made this book possible.

The views expressed by the individuals in this book (or the individuals on the cover) do not necessarily reflect the views shared by the companies they are employed by (or the companies mentioned in this book). The employment status and affiliations of authors with the companies referenced are subject to change.

Inside the Minds:
The Food and Beverage Industry

*Industry Leaders on Manufacturing, Marketing, and
Distributing the Edible Goods that Sell*

CONTENTS

A Glimpse of What Makes "The Wise Owl" Tick

Richard C. Robertson

President and CEO
Wise Foods

The Snacking Segment

Wise Foods is part of the $22 billion snack food industry that concentrates mostly in the area of salty snacks. The US population has a propensity to snack, and the incidence of snacking is increasing as our lifestyles continue to become more hectic. Over time, snacking has gone from a midday 'pick-me-up' to a full-blown meal replacement. Hence, the types of snacks consumed today have changed, as the purpose of snacking has evolved. In this chapter, we will attempt to explore some of the key attributes of a successful manufacturer of snack foods and how to capture the attention of a very demanding consumer with high expectations.

Simply put, snacking is all about fun. Think about the eating occasions associated with snacking and my point becomes clear. At Wise, delivering fun to our consumers is at the forefront of everything we do. We, as most snack manufacturers, strive to provide that fun in a responsible way that addresses all consumer needs.

Wise Foods is one of the larger regional snack food manufacturers in the United States that focuses its distribution in markets in the eastern part of the US. Due to our size, we consider ourselves to be more nimble and responsive to our consumers and customers. Within the salty snack segment there is one very large competitor with extraordinary resources, which requires all others in the industry to find their niches and consumer relevance.

For a snack food manufacturer to be successful, in my estimation there are three critical components: product quality, consumer value and reliability. When consumers seek to snack they are typically looking to satisfy a craving or have a meal replacement of some sort. Whatever the reason, taste is a key decision point and not meeting expectations in this area will likely lead to disappointments by the consumer and the chances of consumers returning to the franchise to enjoy other products becomes less likely. That is why manufacturers need to learn from consumers through comments that are received so that processes and procedures can be reviewed to insure that customer expectations are continually met and taste is satisfied. Beyond taste and product quality, value is an area that is strongly embedded in consumer purchase behavior. Today's consumers are highly educated and are well armed with information. It is in respect to this educated buyer that manufacturers must deliver on the value equation.

Consumers also demand product consistency in their snacks. They expect the product to deliver the same taste and enjoyment time after time. McDonald's created this expectation as they began opening restaurants across the globe. The consumer wants the same taste in their hamburger whether they are in Des Moines or Paris. It may sound simple, however, when you consider that the same product is produced in many different plants across a broad geography, the challenge is large. Even the difference of water purification from city to city can dramatically change the taste and appearance of a product.

Snacks that meet consumer demands in regard to taste, value, and consistency are the ones that will find a following and succeed in the market.

Keeping Product Appeal Fresh

Maintaining the test of time is a brand's greatest challenge. Over the years, the equity of a brand increases or diminishes, depending on how it is managed. One thing is for certain; it is unlikely that it will remain constant. In today's environment, due to the costs of developing a new brand, many manufacturers are leveraging existing brands across different categories to gain quicker recognition by the consumer. The so called 'power brands' have a much higher success rate in new categories than trying to create a totally new brand from scratch.

A brand needs to be 'contemporized' regularly as the consumer need-state changes. Contemporizing products can be done in many different ways – usage, flavors and packaging are three of the more common ways. For snack food manufacturers, usage is clearly defined and it is an area that has the least opportunity. Flavors, packaging and form are probably the more common areas that help contemporize the salty snack segment. Later in this chapter I will be discussing the importance of packaging and how it influences consumer purchasing behaviors. With regards to flavor and forms, recent data on category trends has indicated that the consumer is defining the quality of products in the salty snack arena by the depth of variety. Hence, there is an expectation by the consumer that the brands that offer more choices are likely to be the ones they will purchase over the long term.

The decision to discontinue a product actually begins with the consumer. When a particular product begins to demonstrate consistent, declining sales, despite attempts at refreshing the product, the consumer is beginning to send a message. This could be due to competition from other products or they have found their need state elsewhere. If sales of a particular product continue to decline over a period of time, and are not meeting the financial requirements of the company; the product needs to find its permanent resting place within the company. Failure by the manufacturer to recognize this on a timely basis will likely lead to greater exit costs due to improperly planned costs associated with raw materials, packaging and finished goods.

Bringing a New Product to the Table

The number of new products launched every week in the grocery industry is mind-boggling. It is especially impressive when you remind yourself that the available shelf and display space to carry these items in a supermarket does not grow from week to week. Yet, the consumer has a strong desire to try new products. The cost to develop and subsequently launch new products to meet this consumer demand is significant. Like many things, the process can be shortened and costs reduced by employing less of a process, with little to no consumer research. However, the chance of failure rises significantly, which has a considerable price tag as well. Some of the best ideas never make it in the market because they were missing that one key component that might have been uncovered had proper research been completed.

There are degrees of product innovation: a completely new concept requiring the need to train the consumer in its usage, to a flavor line extension of an existing product. The difference in time and resources will vary considerably depending on the degree of innovation. From concept testing to actually manufacturing the product, the window of time to launch a new product is somewhere between one and two years.

Clearly, a simple line extension is on the lower end of the scale while a completely new concept takes much longer.

In the salty snack segment, consistent new product innovation is one of the keys to success. Consumers today have the opportunity to travel the world and sample new flavors that they seek to replicate at home. They expect manufacturers to keep up-to-date with current trends and provide offerings that are new and different, while still having the 'old favorites' available for their return to reality. I have heard the salty snack consumer defined as 'promiscuous,' whereby they are constantly interested in trying something new, yet they don't want to give up what they have been accustomed to over time. An example might be the flavor 'Chipolte.' Ten years ago, most of us couldn't spell the word. Today we are seeing it appear on products everywhere. A 'Chipolte' flavored potato chip anyone? Yet, will Chipolte replace the 'original' flavor or a brand? I don't think so.

For the last several years, new product innovation has been the growth engine within the salty snack segment. Products that have been in existence for less than a year are driving category growth, while products over a year in market are showing declines. Hence, the salty snack manufacturer that dedicates resources and delivers in this area is likely to be on the winning end of share and revenue growth.

Pointers on Packaging

When it comes to the purchasing of snack foods, there is a high incidence of decision making at the time of purchase, versus a calculated, planned purchase for a specific type or brand with other categories. To bring home the point, think of yourself or your family – how common is it to have listed on your grocery list "potato chips" or "cookies" without indicating a specific brands or flavor? If you are like most, it is very common. As a result of the decision being made at the point of purchase, how a brand communicates on the package to capture the attention of the consumer can be a key to the success of a brand. The image on pack, or product definition, will sell the consumer at a critical time. Clearly, all manufacturers need to follow federal guidelines that require accurate depicting and descriptions of their products. Those manufacturers that truly understand the power of packaging and dedicate appropriate resources will reap significant rewards.

To crystallize my point, think back twenty or so years ago, when supermarkets offered "generic" products. Typically, they were available in a basic black and white package. Their consumer relevance was merely price. Do you see many "generics" on shelves today? Today's private label offerings rival national brands, especially as it relates to packaging. The black and white package did not meet the consumer's need to 'connect' with the product and hence the evolution to today's offerings – which might I add, continues to be a threat to branded manufacturers.

So if a manufacturer wants a consumer connection – packaging plays an enormous role.

Product Distribution

Within the snacking segment, a direct store delivery (DSD) system is the preferred system for product distribution. This system gives direct access to consumers and significantly more control of one's products from manufacturing through to the point of sale. With DSD, sales representatives deliver the product directly to the stores where it is then made available to the consumer. Essentially, a DSD system controls the supply chain all the way through to the point of purchase.

In addition, DSD enables a manufacturer to bring new products to the marketplace very quickly and to promote them more efficiently. For example, a new product launch in a DSD environment is likely to achieve distribution in 90 percent of all stores in the first 90 days of shipment while in a traditional warehouse system, it takes considerably more time. Having an army of people touching and handling only your products, calling on stores two to three times a week, is a real advantage that creates enormous value for one's brands – when properly utilized and configured. Approximately 25 percent of all products sold in the grocery channel are sold through this type of system. Traditionally, it has been those products that are most sensitive to freshness that have utilized a DSD system, however, due to the awareness of the effectiveness of this system, more and more categories have attempted to find DSD solutions for the selling and distribution of their products. A DSD system comes with a significant price tag. In a high velocity segment such as salty snacks, the economics for this type of system are favorable and can deliver extraordinary results.

At Wise Foods, we view our DSD system as a real advantage and a core asset of our company. Besides being merely an expense relating to selling and distribution, it is essentially part of our marketing strategy. It allows us to communicate our message to our consumers, through our customers. We do that through the type of packaging and point-of-sale material that we use to support our brands and the creation of in-store display events.

Leading a Company

Much can be said about the areas of focus of a company leader. I would like to start off by sharing a few thoughts about the importance of understanding one's customer.

It goes without saying, that excellent customer service is an essential component of a successful company – especially in the highly competitive salty snack segment. As CEO of Wise, I subscribe to a philosophy that has been coined "servant leadership." Basically, servant leadership puts an individual in a position in which they seek to serve those to whom they have a responsibility – be it employees or customers. I stress the importance of this philosophy within my management team, as well as with all company employees. By 'raising up' those who diligently try to implement the core strategies of the company day-by-day, customer-by-customer, is certain to create a culture of care that will likely yield desired results. I had the pleasure of working under the leadership of Sam Reed who was the CEO of a former company we worked at and he was the epitome of a servant leader. The culture he helped create was unmatched in the industry and it is no wonder that company sold for extraordinary multiples and the affection for him and his style lives on many years later.

Another important question that I constantly ask of my organization is "Do you know who your customer is?" It is automatically assumed that a 'customer' is one who purchases a product or service from you. But a 'customer' has a much broader definition and it should include any and all with whom one interacts. Don't we really sell ourselves everyday, to everybody? So who is your primary customer? The answering of that question by every individual across the business unit will give everyone a greater purpose.

As CEO, there are essentially three areas that I dedicate my personal involvement on a regular basis. First and foremost, the shareholders have an expectation that I am fully aware of the financial position of the company at all times. I should be capable of answering any of their questions and provide detail to support past performance or future forecasts. This is clearly one of the top fiduciary responsibilities of my office. Second, as I have shared above, customer relationships are a cornerstone of success, and I seek at all times to have a solid and cooperative relationship with a minimum of our top five customers. Ensuring great communication between company leaders and key revenue partners should be an expectation of the highest-ranking officer within a corporation.

Last but not least, be a leader. Outstanding individuals have written volumes on this topic and I do not seek to reinvent what many have already said. The fact of the matter is that there are many more individuals that prefer to follow than lead. People seek leaders. There is a high propensity of individuals who want to follow if they believe in the individual and the message. As history has shown us, leadership talents – and rigorously using them – will energize employees and contribute to the success of any company.

Understanding the Marketplace

The grocery industry has undergone significant changes over the last decade. Today, fifteen percent of groceries are purchased in mass merchandiser outlets – Target, Wal-Mart, K-Mart – and that percentage grows every year. In addition, at last count, 7 percent of groceries were bought in a new trade class called "warehouse club." Ten years ago, there were only a few club stores and they were not even registering with data services. As a result, in the shifting of purchases by the consumer from one channel to another, manufacturing and packaging requirements have changed to accommodate their business model. Those manufacturers that have sat on the sidelines during these changes are likely to be extinct today due to their reluctance to change.

Having strong customer relationships can help in the evolution of one's business. Those relationships can help guide a manufacturer in the changing trends and vice versa. If a customer and manufacturer strategy is not aligned, what are the chances of success? Perhaps one will win at the expense of the other, but how long will it take before they are at odds with one another?

When developing business strategies, it is essential to rely on good industry partners. Establishing a strong partnership with your customer enables you to gain access to perspectives that will prove invaluable as you seek to forecast business trends and consumer preferences, and profitably grow your business.

Keys to Perpetuating Success

There are many directions one can take in answering this age old question; however, I am going to attempt to answer it by focusing on two areas: people and customers. I have found that the easiest way to understand how a company defines itself is by spending time with those who represent it. They are a product of their surroundings and are influenced by the culture they are living. If the company has a clear and concise message that everyone understands and is motivated to live that message all of their working day – it will come out loud and clear in a discussion. I think you would agree that the converse is likely to occur as well, when the message is blurred or just poorly communicated. Wal-Mart does an outstanding job in communicating their message both internally and externally. You may not agree with the message – as you may not agree with others as well – but at least you are clear and understand their strategy and how they perceive they can achieve said strategy. It is simple and well communicated. I recently had the pleasure to attend a supplier summit that included the Presidents/CEOs of manufacturers that sell to Wal-Mart across all categories. As they do in every one of their stores each morning with their associates, they began our meetings with the Wal-Mart cheer in which they stress, "The customer is *Number One!*" Something as simple as that repeated thousands of times a day is sure to bring the behavior that will likely keep their customer coming back. Adding varying degrees of complexity, changing course mid-stream with little communication and understanding by the broad group clouds the direction and makes the rate of success decline rapidly.

So in summary, success is likely with a clearly communicated message that everyone, and I mean everyone, understands.

An equally important component to success is knowing your customer. This applies to the worker at the manufacturing plant as well as the executive in the boardroom. We all need to know who the customer is and how we can best serve him or her. Once everyone is aligned with the same perspective across all departments and levels, there is a very real possibility that your company will be successful. This is one area in which everyone has to *walk-the-walk.*

Food and beverage is not a static industry and companies that want to be on the cutting edge must be prepared to change. Change comes in many different forms: product needs, product attributes, customer base, consumer demands. When a company has the right products and right tools to address changes, it is positioned to grow within the market.

In the snack industry, Wise Foods is in the business of providing fun. We develop, manufacture and distribute products that consumers enjoy. To that end, we have to take into account changes in tastes and market demands. But we always need to recognize that enjoyment is one of the most essential ingredients of our products and the very core of what we do.

Richard C. Robertson is a seasoned Grocery Industry Executive with 27 years of experience predominantly in a Direct Store Delivery (DSD) environment. He is currently President/CEO of Wise Foods, one of the largest regional Salty Snack manufacturers with distribution and production facilities up and down the Eastern Seaboard. Wise Foods has approximately 2400 employees and is a premier manufacturer of both branded and private label products. Wise's brands include: Wise All Natural Potato Chips, Cheez Doodles, Quinlan Pretzels and Bravos

Tortilla Chips and Salsas. The company is headquartered in Kennesaw, GA.

Prior to Wise Foods, Mr. Robertson held the position of Executive Vice President and General Manager of Kellogg Snacks. He became part of the Kellogg Company through the successful acquisition of Keebler Foods in March of 2001. He began his career at Keebler in May of 1977, when he joined in at an entry-level position. During the course of his tenure at Keebler, he rose to the position of Vice President, General Manager of the $1.8 billion DSD biscuit unit at the time of the sale to Kellogg's. He is credited for leading a seamless integration of the Kellogg wholesome snack business into Keebler's Direct Store Delivery system, which included the Nutri-Grain and Rice Krispies Treat brands.

Mr. Robertson is a graduate of the University of Massachusetts, Amherst, MA. He has been an active member of industry associations, including: Grocery Manufacturers Association (GMA) and Snack Food Association (SFA).

Dedication: *I dedicate this chapter to my father – Raymond J. Robertson – who through conviction, passion and determination set an example for me that has forever enriched my life.*

Connecting Your Brand with the Customer

J. Darius Bikoff

Founder and CEO
Energy Brands Inc.

Redefining Bottled Water

The company was founded in 1996, we entered into distribution in 1998 and glacéau **vitamin**water was launched in 2000. Today, glacéau **vitamin**water is the majority of our business, but we also have a rapidly growing brand called glacéau **smart**water. glacéau **smart**water has a line extension called glacéau **smart**water flavors, which is flavored water with no calories.

I entered into this business as a consumer after I noticed that all bottled water had the same imagery of mountains, trees and streams. It was a vague reference to a vague destination, and it didn't make sense to me. None of the products differentiated themselves. In creating glacéau, I wanted a brand that would stand for a fresh new approach to water and was determined to create a product that consumers would find relevant to their lifestyles.

glacéau **vitamin**water has a very special bond with consumers because it redefines bottled water in many ways. The product provides a great tasting, low calorie, healthy hydration option that didn't exist before. The packaging introduced a new modern aesthetic into the consumer goods arena and the personality speaks a new sarcastic language. Thousands of consumers from New York to Los Angeles and everywhere in between call us every day to let us know how strongly they connect with this magical combination.

Customer service is extremely important to any brand and when I started this company, I took every single consumer call myself. *(I don't get out much.)* The person who does that now still reports indirectly to me. *(She doesn't get out much either.)* We call it consumer relations and it isn't really so much about solving or addressing an issue as it is about having a meaningful dialog with that person. When was the last time you called a company? Most people don't often call companies, so when they do, they're really going out of their way. I respect that and think that person has something valuable to tell us. *(Or they're trying to get free stuff.)* Either way, our job is to make it a meaningful dialog, learn everything that we can from that contact and keep the brand relevant by addressing what consumers want.

We've been fortunate to receive incredible editorial coverage and support from the media, which has acted as a third-party endorsement *(vitaminwater for president!)*, and in many ways has been more credible than advertising. Our strongest brand message has come from editors and writers who are passionate about glacéau **vitamin**water, which makes it truly organic publicity.

Meaningful Innovation

Innovation comes from everybody on the team being encouraged to think without being constrained by what we may have the capacity to produce. Instead, we think in terms of what we as consumers want. That's really a whole shift in how beverage companies do business. When you look at the big beverage companies, the products they make are really defined by what they have the capacity to produce. To them, innovation is a line extension, whereas for glacéau **vitamin**water, innovation is about what is relevant and meaningful for consumers. Once we know that then we bring the technology to bear and figure out how to make it. *(Just like on Mr. Wizard's World).*

When considering a new product, we look for a number of different signs. *(What you don't believe in signs?)* The first sign usually comes from consumers *(and my psychic)* telling us what they would like. For example, we began offering our top four SKUs in 32-ounce bottles last year. This larger size was purely a response to consumers who told us they were looking for a bigger gulp of glacéau **vitamin**water – especially during sports. It's the perfect alternative to the sports drinks on the market today, which are salt-based and developed in the 60s, based on old technology. glacéau **vitamin**water is nutrient-based, packed with electrolytes, all natural, and based on the latest technology. *(See, it's a sign!)*

Technology is a very dynamic field, so when there's new nutritional science or new ingredient technology available, we incorporate them into both existing and new products. Continuing to evolve existing products is just as important as creating new ones so we are committed to being the leading edge of ingredient innovation.

While operationally we are very focused on research in the areas of efficacy and clinical trials, we believe just as strongly in being completely engaged with consumers. *(Not engaged to, that would just be wrong.)* It's also about being engaged with our retailers and distributors and always keeping our fingers on the pulse of what's new. We are not only looking at what's new in beverages, but also what's happening with consumer preferences and where they are going. We look at what people are eating today, what's changing in their lifestyles or in their diets and what's changing in the way they behave. *(Basically, we stalk them.)* That is an integral part of our decision-making and product development process. *(Stalking.)*

I think the most important thing for a successful product is relevance. There are probably a lot of great products that don't make it because they're just not relevant to the type of lifestyle consumers are leading today. *(R.I.P. the 8-track.)* In the case of glacéau **vitamin**water, the connection between vitamins and water that makes so much sense also happens to fit into the kind of active and more purposeful lifestyle that people lead today *(well, except for agoraphobics.)* The product attributes are connected on so many levels with that type of relevance, whether it's that it provides healthier benefits while still being great tasting, or that it has iconic packaging that is also extremely portable. *(Or, that people get thirsty.)*

You Get What You Pay For

glacéau **vitamin**water participates in the premium segment and while our products are premium-priced, they also offer a tremendous amount of added value in the way of nutrient enhancement and great tasting, healthier hydration. We've seen over and over again that consumers are willing to pay a little more for premium products as long as the value-added proposition is there. *(Like how $100 dollar sneakers might help you jump higher...Um, no.)*

At the same time, we use much higher quality ingredients than commercial beverage manufacturers. For example, we use crystalline fructose as a sweetener, which is much more expensive than high fructose corn syrup which has been linked to childhood obesity. We use only natural ingredients, and we incorporate meaningful levels of nutrients. Natural flavors and natural colors obviously make for a slightly more costly product. *(Naturally.)*

When you buy a commercial beverage, only a very small fraction of what you pay is being spent on actual ingredients, whereas when you buy a bottle of glacéau **vitamin**water, almost all of your money is going toward ingredients. When you buy a Pepsi, you're really paying for the millions they paid Britney Spears to do a commercial. When you buy a bottle of glacéau **vitamin**water, you are paying for our senior vice president of operations, Dr. Carol Dollard, who holds a Ph.D in food science, to go out and find you the highest quality ingredients you could possibly be putting in your body. That's the difference. (*Well sure, there are a few other differences between Britney and Carol, but we'll save that for another time.*)

Show Me the Money

I'd like for glacéau **vitamin**water to be the best brand it can be. I want it to continue to connect with consumers from five to eighty-five, and to be a hydration option for anyone who wants to lead a healthier, more purposeful lifestyle. If we can do that and offer all of these options to consumers that didn't exist before, then that's success.

While the company has experienced exponential growth since its inception, we don't discuss our margins – we're a private company. (*If I told you, I'd have to kill you.*) What I can say is that we offer very healthy margins for all of our distribution and retail partners while still being at a reasonable price point for a premium product to the consumer.

Instead of focusing on growing revenues (*we're not a financially driven organization*), we are a brand driven organization, which means that our philosophy is that if we are good stewards of the brand, and if we do everything we should to build the brand in a way that is relevant for consumers and efficient from a production and management point of view, then the financial rewards will come as a result. So far, that has worked. We've had a significant amount of competition come after us from Pepsi, Coke and Cadbury, and they all failed. Today we pretty much dominate the enhanced water category. *(Insert evil cackle here.)*

Velocity is how we measure the success of the products and the company. We know that we've done something right when consumers are buying the product. In a lot of ways, this whole experiment happened because I wanted the product for myself. My hope was that if I wanted it, other people would too. Now, more than two million people a day buy a bottle of glacéau **vitamin**water and that lets me know that I'm on the right track. *(You like me, you really like me!)*

Growing Up the Hard Way

It is extremely important to work closely with our distributors *(even though I'm claustrophobic)* to build the brand within their territory. We view distributors as partners. It's really up to us to build the brand.

We started out as a natural foods company so we were predominantly in the natural foods stores: chains like Whole Foods and Wild Oats. More recently, we've expanded into more mainstream distribution, and today we're available everywhere from Stop n' Shop and King Kullen in the east to Ralph's and Safeway in the west. We've really expanded much more significantly into mainstream distribution over the last couple of years. *(Next up: Vitaminwater, The Movie.)*

It's hard to say what retailers look for in a product. *(Retailer seeks beverage that enjoys long walks on the beach and sushi.)* The best retailers look for innovation and a consumer connection because they want to serve their community and offer their consumers something relevant. On the other hand, some retailers just want the products that they're going to get the most money for from the manufacturer. If all you see are Coke or Pepsi products, that's because they have a so-called exclusive contract that precludes other beverages from being sold at that retailer. People don't want some big company dictating what they can drink. *(Orwell's 1984, hello?)* It's certainly not what I want. Retailers may get a lot of money up front for those deals, but I think they lose a lot of credibility in the end.

There are lots of products that are successful in the natural foods channel and never cross over into the mainstream. It's really a matter of scale and whether or not that scale is adequate to sustain the business. When I first started in this business, my vision was to be purely a natural foods company. Now, I'd like to be more of a crossover/mainstream brand, following in the footsteps of products like energy bars, organics and soy *(and pop/country sensation Faith Hill.)*

When the Stop n' Shop buyer calls you and says, "I've been drinking glacéau **vitamin**water for the past six months in my yoga studio and I want it in the store," that's usually a pretty good sign *(see, another sign!)* that it's time to cross over to the larger stores. You have to look for cues in the market that consumers want you to be in a certain place. Not every product has to be everywhere, but once in a while, for a brand like glacéau **vitamin**water, it is appropriate if that's what consumers want. When we do mainstream, we still do it with style.

The Discomfort Zone

The most challenging aspect of this industry is probably embracing the fact that every day is a new experience, not just for me, but also for the entire organization. We're a young company that has grown very rapidly. For the most part, we've hired people who are passionate and enthusiastic about the brand and not necessarily because they have been in the industry for many years. As an organization, we are about embracing change and whatever challenges might come tomorrow that we haven't had to confront in the past. That's what makes it the most fun. We stay fresh by being consumers and listening to consumers. We don't produce anything that we wouldn't want to consume ourselves. *(That's why we don't make brussel sprouts.)*

We teach our staff that it's okay to do things in a new or different way. *(Hey, the French put mayonnaise on their fries.)* Much of our approach to the business is different. For instance, in an effort to meet the demand for glacéau **vitamin**water on the west coast, we closed the New York office and flew the entire company out to California. We immersed ourselves in the local scene so that we could be a California company, not a New York company trying to succeed in California.

There's been a tremendous consolidation in the industry and the big beverage companies like Coke, Pepsi and Cadbury have more or less created an atmosphere where entrepreneurial products from small companies really can't get into distribution. Ultimately, that's bad for consumers and I think it is part of why people are so passionate about glacéau **vitamin**water. *(But we still can't explain the whole trucker hat thing.)*

I definitely think the trend toward a healthier lifestyle is going to become more meaningful. I don't really see any end in sight for that. I think people are going to continue to drink more bottled water and that they are going to continue to look for a bridge from carbonated soft drinks and new age beverages like Snapple to water. Our mission is to make glacéau **vitamin**water that bridge. *(A bridge over troubled waters, if you will. Pardon the pun.)*

If It Was Easy, Everybody Would Do It

The advice I tend to give is to not listen to the experts because all of the experts told me that glacéau **vitamin**water would never succeed. Today those same experts are saying that glacéau **vitamin**water will be the next billion-dollar brand in the industry, so I think that you have to follow your own instincts and be committed to innovation. My golden rules for business are to try to do something that you are passionate about, create something that doesn't already exist, build a team of smart people and don't give up. *(Oh and hang a bunch of those motivational posters up all around the office. That really seems to help.)*

During a New York City water shortage in the early 1990s, Mr. J. Darius Bikoff realized that there was a void in the water industry as he searched his local market for a better alternative to tap water and a more exciting alternative to bottled water. Further research and his knowledge of packaging prompted Mr. Bikoff's quest to create better water, which led to the vision of energy brands, a company that would forever change the bottled-water industry.

Throughout his career, Mr. Bikoff, Founder/CEO of Energy Brands Inc. (parent company of glacéau vitaminwater and glacéau smartwater) excelled as an entrepreneur. He began his career in the metals industry in 1983 as a packaging supplier to top beverage companies worldwide. From there, Mr. Bikoff moved into the bottled-water industry where he built brands that have since become iconic categories.

Formed in 1996, Energy Brands is committed to creating biologically better water so that people feel good about what they drink. Since its inception, Energy Brands has been recognized as the pioneer and leader in the enhanced water category. The company currently carries two lines of enhanced water products: glacéau smartwater™ and glacéau vitaminwater™.

Mr. Bikoff has a history of innovative breakthroughs, including the creation of the patented 20-ounce sportsbottle cap in 1991, which is in a number of museum collections including the Smithsonian.

Mr. Bikoff graduated from Colgate University with a Bachelor of Arts. He was awarded Brandweek's "Marketers of the Next Generation" in 2000, and Crain's "New York's Top Entrepreneurs" in 2001. In February 2003, Mr. Bikoff was featured on the cover of Fortune Small Business for an article that profiled his entrepreneurship in the bottled-water industry and his company. Mr. Bikoff was named as one of this year's Fast Company "Fast 50."

Dedication: *To Mike Repole, our very own "King of Queens," without whom my secret to success might still be a secret and I'd be selling water out of my trunk.*

Taking Quality and Innovation to Creamy New Heights

Thomas Kunz

President and CEO

The Dannon Company, Inc.

Current and Future Consumer Issues

The food and beverage industry is coming under increasing scrutiny from all sorts of interest groups. The obesity concern, which has become a major issue for the food and beverage industry, will create a host of different trends. Some of those trends will be based on solid science; most will be based on hearsay. We will see countless self-proclaimed scientists and specialists issue books and write articles.

Today, the massive variety of micro trends confuses consumers about what to believe and what not to believe. It will be quite difficult for the food industry to predict which of those micro trends, if any, will actually emerge as a mainstream trend. The Atkins low-carb trend, for example, has exploded recently. All it took was an article in the *New England Journal of Medicine* saying the diet is as effective as or more effective than the classic low-fat diet.

The food industry in general and specific representatives of the food industry will be put on "public trials," and there will be forces that try to blame obesity, diabetes, and other health-related problems on the food industry. The industry is a handy scapegoat, and it is much easier to blame the food industry than to blame the lack of parental guidance, for example. The food industry has become more alert in its effort to understand what is going on everywhere.

In the last ten years in the United States, "healthful food" meant low-fat food. It was a very simplistic way of looking at something much more complex. We need to look at how much nutritional value a food has per calorie. These things will become more important, and obviously we believe we are well positioned. I think our products taste great, are healthful, and have a good health image. That is why I believe we have a bright future.

Requisites: Taste and Convenience

The number one thing a company in the food industry has to deliver with a product is taste. If the product does not taste good, not much else matters. You may be moderately successful with something that does not taste particularly good, but has a compelling health story. Sustained long-term success, however, means taste is a must. If you can add a meaningful health benefit to great taste, you have a winner.

And never underestimate the importance of convenience in the United States. If you look at the big success stories in food, they are all highly convenient. There are whole categories that are built pretty much on convenience. A very good example of this is Kraft Lunchables.

An aspect of convenience is availability. In certain food industry segments, product availability is actually more important to the consumer than brand. Take the bottled water category: It is all about availability. If you are thirsty and want to drink a bottle of water, you don't care about the brand of water as long as the water is available. Coke has built an empire on this factor.

New Products and the Window of Profitability

Our R&D process is not revolutionary. It starts with a concept phase, which is followed by an executive committee meeting, where we approve what we call a basis for interest. We then have a definition phase and the development phase. Then we implement and launch. After each phase we make a very deliberate executive committee decision to go ahead or not.

We know within certain limits from the outset how we will price a product. We test different price levels, noting consumer reaction, and then determine the price. Occasionally other elements determine the pricing. If you open a new category, the instinct is to charge as much as you can. Sometimes, however, you may want to decide to charge less to keep competition from launching right away. We call this managing the window of profitability. If you leave it open too wide, you make it too easy for competition to slip in at the lower price, yet still be very profitable. This may be particularly relevant when you don't have a high technological barrier.

Cold Retail Realities

One of the principal determinants of the way we operate is that our product has a short life – about 40 days from the time it's manufactured to the time it has to be consumed. This makes it a very fast business, and one of our most difficult challenges is to avoid being out of stock: If we fill the yogurt shelf this morning, it may be empty again by evening.

Constant Innovation and Constant Quality Improvement

If you stand still and do not innovate in this industry, you are history. In Dannon's case, innovation is a big part of growing revenues and profits.

Innovation is not only the development of new products, but keeping old products fresh and making them better every year. The product that is the best we can do today is not necessarily the best we can do tomorrow. Ideally, if we have made a re-launch and improvement of a product, we should start the following day working on the next improvement for that product.

There is room for improvement in the yogurt category in the United States. Per capita consumption in the United States is about 10 percent to 15 percent of that in Europe. The yogurt category of the last five years has changed tremendously. The number of new offerings is quite astonishing. This is paying dividends in a very dynamic market growth of about 10 percent per year. Our mission is to find a way to be as big in the yogurt category in the United States as we are in Europe.

The Role of the CEO

Quality plays an extremely important role in my job as Dannon's CEO. I need to make sure the organization at large understands that the concept of quality is not something to execute when it is convenient, but that it is truly at the foundation of long-term success. I strive to create an atmosphere in the company where working with poor quality is simply not an option. The work quality of every individual is of the utmost importance to the success of the company.

Secondly, making the organization work as a whole is key. I may have the best quality people, but if they don't work together in an efficient way, the company will not be successful. Avoiding the development of functional silos is therefore one of the most important missions that I have.

The third important part of my job as CEO is to stoke the fire, keep it burning and make sure that we improve every day. There is great truth in the saying that success breeds failure: The greater the success, the greater the danger of complacency. Striking the right balance between celebrating success and understanding the dangers ahead is both important and difficult.

We are very specifically in a race for market leadership with our competitor, Yoplait. A very competitive view of this situation permeates the organization. This creates both advantages and disadvantages. The advantage is that there is great clarity and simplicity of what we want to secure: market leadership. The danger is that the organization becomes too focused on the competitor and lets its actions be determined by the competitor as opposed to focusing on our own development.

One last thought – when I entered the food service industry, one of the things that struck me most was if you sell detergents, diapers, or such, your market is pretty much determined. This is not so in the food industry. We have to constantly remind ourselves not to get caught up too much in our category. Our true market and opportunities are not defined by the size of the yogurt market, but by what the human body can ingest. This is the difference between share-of-stomach versus share-of-market – in the food business, you are not really limited.

Thomas Kunz joined Groupe Danone in 1990. As Dannon CEO and President, Mr. Kunz is Senior Executive VP for the U.S. and Canada dairy product activities. Prior to this position, he was general manager of Bagley S.A., a Groupe Danone subsidiary in Argentina. He started as director marketing in Munich, Germany and five years later was appointed general manager of Danone Mexico. Prior to joining Groupe Danone, Mr. Kunz worked at Procter and Gamble in brand management for seven years. As a graduate of Saint Gall University in Switzerland, Mr. Kunz holds a master degree in Economics

When Consumers Demand,
Cash Flows

Christopher J. New

CEO
Galaxy Nutritional Foods Company

Tackling the Avalanche

Consumers are drawn to Galaxy Foods because there is an avalanche of negative health trends in the world, like obesity, particularly among children. Our company provides solutions for healthful eating and turns those solutions into consumable products. We have non-dairy alternatives to conventional cheese products – sliced, shredded, chunk/block, string cheese, sour cream, and butter, to name a few. Our Veggie Brand Products taste great and are lactose-free, cholesterol-free, contain no transfatty acids and are low fat. It is a solution to a problem that is growing at an unprecedented rate.

Someone once taught me that marketing is the art of putting your products in front of avalanches. The avalanche is a negative health trend, and we are now getting in front of that trend with a product that consumers look for, want, and more strongly, are now demanding.

Making a Difference: The Premium Quality Model

Fundamentally, within the dairy context of conventional cheese-type products, very few people are capable of attempting to do what we do – and do effectively.

We have the first-mover advantage. We thought of it first; we did it first; and we invented processes that deliver high-quality products across a wide spectrum of needs, so we have that insulation in the marketplace. We have done it based on what I call the premium-quality model. This is how our company actually builds margin and is able to translate that into cash flow.

Think of an analog clock. At the top is twelve o'clock – and that's where superior product quality is built and made available to consumers. At three o'clock, you have superior market share. We have an 87 percent share of the retail grocery market in our category and a 55 percent share of the natural foods market. Since consumers have a superior experience with our product, we get higher market share.

At six o'clock, at the bottom of the clock, we charge more for our products than our competition. We have a superior pricing model where we are at a 30 percent premium versus most of our competition. We are actually priced parity to 10 percent premium versus conventional cheese. Since consumers get an exceptional experience for our product, we are able to charge more for it.

That takes us to nine o'clock, which is where our superior margin lives. Higher pricing and better market share lead to higher margin. We are the low-cost provider on many of the products we provide, so we deliver superior margins, which then lead us back to twelve o'clock, where we can choose to invest that margin back in the business for the betterment of the product, for the consumer, and for the bottom line – the shareholder.

That premium quality model, as we move around clockwise at a faster and faster rate, creates insulation and thus enables us to be better than our competition. In many regards, we are like an intellectual property company. We don't patent our technologies and our processes, but we have created manufacturing processes and R&D trade secrets that allow us to do things better than other companies.

Product Success Factor: Consumer Need-State Model

Taste is king. I focus our company on consumer preferences and demands via a consumer need-state model. Consumers think about products and benefits in terms of their need states. A need state, for example, identifies who the consumer is, when they use the product, where they use it, and how they use it. So from that we can target the proper consumer, with a product that's optimal for a specific time of day, and keyed into a particular usage occasion and place for consumption. These all link together to form our consumer need-state model.

For example, a need state could indicate how filling or satiating the product is, and how much nutrition it should deliver to be appealing to a large group of consumers. Is it convenient or portable? Is it good for on the go or at home consumption? As you begin to combine these types of benefits into bundles, you are combining sub consumer need states into bigger and potentially more powerful, compelling consumer market needs and opportunities. The better you do that, the more likely your product will be successful in the marketplace. And the closer to being truly unique your product is, the better. Ours, again, is the first non-dairy alternative to many conventional cheese products. We combine superior benefit with all the functionality in the existing category, and we do that with a great-tasting product that is unique.

Uniqueness, great taste, availability, and visibility to the consumer, at price value – which doesn't mean cheap, but the price consumers are willing to pay for the product and resultant benefits– that's what it takes for a product to be successful.

R&D for Product Launch: Three-step Process

Much of our R&D is proprietary and therefore confidential. But I can share what we do before we introduce any product in the marketplace. The process has three steps.

The first step: Do we want to do it? We create a basis for interest, or BFI. In that basis for interest, we identify strategically whether we want to do something new or not. Then we go through a questioning process: How big would this idea be? What is the rationale for thinking the consumer might be interested? What need state would this product fulfill? What benefits does this bring to our trade partners – retailers and distributors, for example? What impact would this have on us from a financial perspective, from a cash-flow perspective, and from an operations perspective? Do we think it's a good idea?

We estimate pricing, margin and volume. Then we prioritize, for example: "We have fifteen projects that are in the BFI stage, the first stage of our process to market. Do we want to do all fifteen, or do we want to do only three of them?" We decide that issue against our business goals, degree of difficulty and most importantly the impact on cash flow from operations.

The second step is called feasibility. In feasibility, we don't discuss whether we *want* to do this anymore; we decide whether we *can* do it – *before* we communicate to our sales team and to our trade partners that we *will* do it. This phase requires a large degree of intellectual capital, time and resources from our organization and we insist upon rigorous evaluation and commitment to understanding our capabilities.

Step three is commercialization. We know we want to do something; we know we can do it; and we actually put the plan in place to implement it. We set our final target ship dates and what the actual portfolio will look like.

This whole process can take anywhere from one week to eighteen months, depending on the complexity of the project and the newness of the idea. The process ensures three important points:

1. We maintain confidentiality.
2. We are always convinced we can deliver on what we say we can do because we've done the scope and feasibility legwork with rigor.
3. We prioritize our projects to meet our portfolio and our growth needs in a very organized fashion that provides visibility to our management team and our board.

Product Development: Preponderance of Positives

Product development gets down to the fundamental need states. Consumers' need states change and evolve a bit, but using food as an example, the number one reason people eat food – on a primal level – is that food has calories, and calories translate into energy, which builds up to nutrition, the ultimate benefit. It's good for people; it's healthful; it will make them feel good. We build basic products that fit into the normal lifestyle needs of consumers: They're portable; they're easy to open; they taste great; and their vitamins and minerals benefit healthy functioning. Our products have more than just the absence of negatives – they have a preponderance of positives.

You need a business model, from a food perspective, that lasts for a long time, one that your organization can institutionalize and repeat with competency. And then it becomes a matter of incorporating incremental benefits and tweaking your product or line – extending your offerings by creating new items along the way that meet more and more of the consumers' needs.

I have been in the packaged food and beverage industry for the past twenty years, and I introduced new products when I was an assistant product manager at a paper manufacturing company during the beginning of my career that are still in the marketplace today. These products share common characteristics to almost every new product or brand I've built during my career; they have the same brand fundamental: They hit a very large universe of consumers and had a compelling benefit, and the company delivered well on them; they aligned precisely with the company's core competencies, and the products' success feeds on itself over and over.

If you manage your consumer portfolio against compelling consumer needs and keep a sharply focused eye on the financial metrics, controllables, organizations capabilities and stability, then you should have a solid, winning proposition.

Business Plan Per Product

We do brand portfolio planning and managing. I try to market our brand to marketplaces, not to channels of distribution. For example, on a broad level basis I want to market to the state of Florida, not just to Publix stores in Florida. As we follow this market plan, we create an umbrella brand, which transcends the natural food set and the grocery set. The product can also go into Wal-Mart, and it can be sold in convenience stores, as well as drug stores, mass clubs, and Food Service outlets.

Our brand crosses those channels. I look to create and manage premium brands that can achieve critical mass, that enable me to then market and advertise the brand so that I can get my message to the consumer by pulling it through the different channels of distribution in the marketplace.

The goals for each of our products are to be the best-tasting product in the class we compete in and to have a score versus our conventional cheese competitor that is within 25 percent of their score on taste and price value. We also strive to achieve a level of availability to consumers of 50 percent to 60 percent distribution in the country.

From a revenue perspective, we would like our portfolio – our company – to be able to grow to a critical mass of at least $150 million within the next three to five years.

Consumer Testing to Build Portfolio and Price Products

Product concept fit testing helps products clear some hurdles. A product concept fit test, conducted by BASES Company, are simulated marketing tests with standard norms for definitely-would-buy and probably-would-buy scores, called, respectively, top-box and top-two-box. I look for food and beverage products that score, at a minimum, 35 percent to 40 percent top-box and 80 percent in the top-two-box, both before trial and after trial. After I review and understand this data and the diagnostic date, I decide whether to scrap, rework, or to launch the product in the marketplace.

Another model we use is a bit more micro and rifle in the approach, which has the effect of getting our product out into the marketplace into a specific channel and a limited geography in a very quick timeframe. It allows us to practice and test with consumers, live and onsite, in stores and in homes of consumers. As the brand starts to build distribution and velocity – velocity is how fast the product turns in the stores we are in on dollar and unit bases – we work with the accounts to understand what their velocity threshold is and then build in consumer marketing campaigns that drive our brands velocity, to make sure we meet that retailer's benchmark.

The idea behind the testing is to build a portfolio of products that enable us to have a base franchise and then leverage this brand to extend into new segments, which are/can be new consumers, new usage occasions, new times of day for the product, and different demographics and age groups. We want a brand that, through the products within its portfolio, can appeal to an older consumer, because the population is aging and our consumer franchise skews toward 45-year-olds and older. At the same time, however, we want to be sure we have another segment in our portfolio, for example our sliced cheese and string cheese that appeal to younger consumers. We start getting young mothers with children in the household into our franchise, and we expand our overall household penetration.

Through competitive assessment/evaluation and BASES testing, we evaluate what price consumers are willing to bear for our products. We price the product at a gap from our premium competition. That gap is anywhere from 5 percent to 30 percent. Then we check the velocity: How does the product sell on that basis? Next, we drive costs out of our system and out of our product to achieve market share.

I've always believed the best way to develop a pricing strategy is to follow Peter Drucker's principle: One should practice price-based costing, not cost-based pricing. Set the price that generates compelling velocity and market share, and then drive the costs out of your product proposition in order to enhance margin growth.

Quantity Per Serving: What Satisfies?

As you look at price-value, first, you check the competition to see where they are. But if you are a leader in the industry, as we have been, you often have to make the quantity-per-serving decision without waiting for the competition's decision. Again, we usually go to the consumer to gain an understanding of what amount of product content satisfies their need.

I spent a great deal of time in the beverage industry working for Tropicana, a division of PepsiCo. If the product in question was for refreshment, we asked questions that gave us insight such as, "How many ounces do you drink before you feel refreshed?" If the product was for satiation, we asked, "How many ounces do you drink before you feel full?" Obviously we were much more technical in our research approach but you get the picture.

I use this questioning now, in the food industry. It's fairly standard. According to the FDA, a standard serving of cheese is 19 grams, and this creates the basis for which all nutritionals per serving are determined. So the question becomes, how many slices go into the package, based on the pricing strategy we want to offer the consumer.

We might want to offer our slices, for example, on a per gram basis at a slight premium against our competition. But in terms of total price point on the shelf, we might be lower than the competition because we have fewer slices in the package.

This is a pricing game and a promotional game. And we compete based on product quality, trial and error in market, as well as some price modeling.

Advertising and Marketing to Consumers

The best way to market our products is to have an integrated marketing plan that provides for awareness-building vehicles like print advertising in *Prevention* magazine and *Woman's Day*. We may combine a coupon with the print ad so you actually get some trial along with awareness and do in-store sampling, where consumers actually taste and try our product before they are asked to purchase it. And we often hand out another coupon at that point to help secure trial.

The other significant factor in moving our business is on-pack coupons and point of sale material in the store. They create an incentive for our current users to buy more products and attract new users to buy our products for the first time. We use several in-store promotional vehicles, as well, such as feature advertising and point-of-sale advertising, which allows consumers to see and identify the product and its benefits.

Articulating the benefits derived from using the product is at least as important as pointing out its features. Rather than just telling someone the cheese product is made with soy, we tell them that eating a diet that contains 25 grams of soy per day can lower cholesterol and lead to a healthier heart. We like to talk about the benefits.

Keeping Older Products Fresh in Consumers' Minds

The revitalization of our core franchise means we have room for tremendous distribution growth, so we are not even close to the problems of having a mature brand and getting the consumer re-excited about it. All brands have lifecycles that transcend infancy through maturity in the marketplace. When a brand reaches maturity, often the financial decisions/strategy changes from harvest to milking. One goes from reinvesting in the brand to taking the money from the mature brand and reinvesting it into another or taking the money to the bottom line. As I mentioned, our brands are still in the high growth, exciting and appealing portion of their lifecycle with consumers. We are investing for growth and expansion, not milking for profit.

But we do like to keep our packaging and benefit communication fresh. One way we do this is by switching some of the benefits featured on the packaging. One quarter, we will talk about great taste. The next quarter, we will use package flags and talk about how are products are good for low carbohydrate diets. The next quarter we point out that it contains soy. The next time, we mention that it's lactose- and cholesterol-free. We try to rotate our key hierarchy of benefits through our advertising and promotion packaging to the consumer. All the time keeping the single-minded benefit of great tasting nutrition in front of consumers.

And we stay up with the trends. If we see a need to add ingredients or fortification when there is a new trend in eating habits, we try to incorporate that into our base brand. If it is meaningful to consumers, they can learn about it and take advantage of it.

When to Pull the Product

When sales data warrant doing so, I pull products that aren't contributing their share to the company's cash flow. We do that on two fronts.

I look at the internal constraints on production, purchasing, and cash availability in terms of carrying the SKU (stock-keeping unit, or product) in my warehouse and producing it.

The second thing I look at is raw consumer demand. With no promotion or advertising, does this particular product have enough vitality or consumer velocity on the shelf to meet the minimum hurdles of the retailer? If it doesn't, then I pull it from the marketplace myself through a category management approach, and I replace it with another product that will sell faster and provide me with a better margin and cash flow.

Partnership Considerations

Because we market to different channels of distribution, we use both distributors and a direct to warehouse basis. We go through the warehouse fundamentally to our retail grocery business, and we go through distributors, for the most part, to get to the food service and natural foods outlets.

INSIDE THE MINDS

Our goal, obviously, is to partner with the best distributors and best retail accounts. That gets us what I call availability and visibility for consumers. It's all about how many points of availability there are for consumers to be able to reach out and touch our products and have opportunities to purchase them.

Our products have to be chilled – kept cold – throughout the entire distribution process. We use chilled warehousing and chilled trucks, for example, to reach the marketplace. Those constraints define whom we use for distribution partners.

Our biggest channel is our retail grocery channel, followed by our natural food set. I believe there is huge opportunity for growth in food service. We are starting to do more business with Wal-Mart and Wal-Mart food centers, which act very much like the grocery channel.

We do not have heavy penetration through convenience stories and drug stores yet, and we are looking to enter into the club mass merchandiser in a bigger way once our franchise is entrenched on the retail side.

Retailers want to make sure there is differentiation in competition. They want evidence and proof from the manufacturer that there is a consumer reason for a product's existence and that the product tastes good. They also look at the dollar velocity, or dollars per point of distribution, that the product will generate and the dollar ring for the retailer per purchase. That translates into raw dollars, as well as margin, for them. At the most basic level, the issues are uniqueness, and space-to-sales ratio and profitability.

We are in the produce department in retail grocery stores. Produce departments are looking for excitement and new things to merchandize and for a way to bring uniqueness to the produce area. And we offer that. We have a good shelf life, and we are new, made with soy, low carbohydrate and very hot on the new-age trends. We give the produce department something to talk about for its future.

We provide every retail store we approach with a suggested plan-a-gram, which shows how the product should be set on the shelf, how it should be priced, and what SKUs they should carry. We also provide merchandising materials – shelf strips, point-of-sale ads, shelf danglers, and ideas on how to get cross-promotions on displays.

Again, taste wins the game. After the consumer proves our superior product quality in trials, the retailer will give us increasingly more shelf space because our brand performs better than those of our competitors.

We typically win shelf space through our ultimate benefit, which is great taste, but then we feature the key benefits on our packaging and in our communication message to consumers. That process enables our products to dominate our competition.

The Importance of Customer Service

You are only as good as your last delivery to your customer. Customer service is critical. I joined the Galaxy Nutritional Foods company in September 2001, bringing with me, from Tropicana, a mindset of extremely high-quality customer service.

The metrics you can use to determine the quality of your customer service are:

- *Order-fill rate:* Out of 100 orders, how many did you fill 100 percent correctly with all the right SKUs and the right amounts?
- *Case-fill rate:* Out of 100 cases ordered, how many cases did you actually ship?
- *On-time delivery:* When the customer called and asked for your truck to arrive in San Diego on Thursday at 10 a.m., was it there?

Those are the three metrics we use. At Galaxy Nutritional Foods in September 2001, we had a 17 percent order-fill rate and a case-fill rate of under 50 percent – both abysmal. We didn't even track on-time delivery because we could hardly deliver products at all.

Now, a mere two years later, we maintain an order-fill rate and a case-fill rate of 99.9 percent to 100 percent, and we are climbing into the 90s for on-time delivery.

Customers penalize you if you don't fulfill against those three different metrics. They will deduct from your invoice; they will penalize you with lump sum cash payments; and they will kick your products off the shelf. They don't take kindly to poor customer service. It is critically important to focus on the customer.

There is a saying in our industry: If you think there is someone more important than the customer, think again.

Growth, Revenues, Profits

Proper planning prevents poor performance. I have a strategy here called "Grow the core, then add more." Concentrate on your core franchise, your core SKUs that make up 80+ percent of your business. Develop a go-to-market plan that ensures those products will grow at the rate you need them to grow to fulfill your objectives for your shareholders or your board.

Assume you are trying to grow 10 percent per year in net revenue. You build your base SKUs to fulfill at least 75 percent to 80 percent of that growth. Then you layer on key initiatives to fill the gap for the remaining growth to get you to a total of 10 percent. Load into your plan those key initiatives – and then develop additional key initiatives that you keep out of your plan, but obviously go way beyond achieving that 10 percent growth rate.

You manage all that on a puts-and-takes basis every week of the year, month by month, quarter by quarter. You know, then, from your planning assumptions, that at a specific time, something is supposed to happen, the amount of revenue you get if it does happen, and who is accountable for making it happen. You set up teams internally to manage each of those key priorities and make sure your sales team has very clear visibility, from the bottom up, of what they need to do to deliver their business.

I manage these details weekly. It is my responsibility to make sure that resources are in place, that cash is available to execute the programs, that the production facility gets its work done, and that Wall Street is satisfied with our performance. All those different variables come into play, but the most important is mapping out your long-term strategic plan, identifying your growth rates, and then building tiered plans – from the bottom up and from the top down – that link your efforts to the numbers you are trying to deliver.

We try to achieve on an ongoing basis 45 percent to 55 percent gross margin. Gross margins at that level mean ours is a top-performing company in the industry, again, assuming that translates all the way down through our positive cash flow.

Cost of goods, labor, and transportation are our highest costs. Our selling and marketing expense is what we call controllable, but we don't truly control transportation costs – we manage activities that impact them. Cost of goods is the largest component of our overall costs, and obviously we have overhead with our plant facility on top of our cost of goods model.

Managing Changing Challenges

Challenges for us change every six months to a year. Since I have been with the company, the biggest challenge has been securing enough working capital that we can buy the ingredients, get the products made, and ship them to our customers. Now that we are through that, and our customer fill rates are in the 100 percent range, our biggest challenge is how to grow top-line profitably: How do we get those key initiatives into the marketplace at the right time and generate the net revenue, control expense and therefore deliver positive cash flow.

On a broader basis, beyond the operational elements, I think quality, again, is our number one concern. We need to constantly be thinking of making the products with the absolute highest quality going forward, so we actually have a product that tastes great and that consumers will demand when faced with choices.

And those efforts are creating a broader marketplace. Our niche is our orientation to health-driven consumers, so our next biggest challenge is to make our products more mainstream and make them more available to mainstream consumers.

CEO Metrics: Six Key Focal Points

As a CEO, I develop metrics that enable me to manage weekly against whatever happens. There are six key items I focus on, all of them under the umbrella focus of positive operating cash flow. Cash flow is life. Everything else is just details.

First is positioning. I have to make sure that I am steering the ship from a positioning perspective and in a strategic direction that is appropriate for the creation of shareholder value.

The second is making sure the products we make are actually available to our consumers – that they can find them on shelves in the store, and that they are visible to consumers.

The third item I focus on is making sure our overall go-to-market model becomes consumer-driven, not trade-pushed. Every action I take internally, in addition to cash flow management, attempts to create a consumer-pull model. That is where I develop a marketing mix that includes advertising, coupon and sampling opportunities, shelf management and those things that pull the product to the consumers, rather than only pushing it through the trade channel.

My fourth focus is on cost and management. I work from the principle of 4Cs: customers, consumers, costs, and competition. I focus on those four things to make sure the go-to-market model is right and that I am driving hard to eliminate costs and competition. That gives me the 40 percent to 50 percent margin I mentioned. That is supply chain management, fixing the products mix, improving efficiencies in the plant, and maintaining customer fill rates.

The fifth key item is looking for strategic partnerships for areas, either geographically or by product, that would better position us for success than going it alone. It's a little of the build-or-buy decision matrix.

Finally, as far as our international business is concerned, the presence of soy in products is exploding throughout Europe. Lacking the resources and time to focus on growing that business myself, I entered into a strategic partnership with Fromageries Bel, the second largest cheese company in Europe. They will distribute, sell, and market our technology in Europe – which takes me to my final focus point.

The last of my top six focus points is strategic partnerships – concentrating on building a more capable and diverse organization with improved business systems. My job, as I said, is to make sure that the resources are available to our organization, that when applied appropriately will generate increasing shareholder value. To accomplish this, one has to fill critical leadership positions with strong, diverse people and successfully implement business systems that provide support to our organization and allow us to get to market faster, more profitably, more effectively, with high quality – or all of the above. I work with my CFO, Salvatore Furnari, on these focal points to figure out how we can generate more cash flow from operations.

Surviving Marketplace Turmoil

To survive in this constantly changing marketplace, first and foremost, my strategy is to be out in front or be run over.

We lead as a company. We believe that as the category leader with 87 percent market share, it is our obligation to grow the categories and the segments we compete in.

We stay on top of trends. Key management members participate in several think tanks in the industry. There is a need within our organization for diverse candidates who have experience in our industry and bring thought leadership. Our sharp focus on the growth of operating cash flow forces us to have a strategic map that tells us what we should do and what we shouldn't do. We review that broad map every year, and we translate that long-range strategic plan into an annual operating plan and break down that operating plan into its key components of growth – base and incremental growth. This is again done via the waterfall analysis I talked about earlier: Your baseline = $x\%$ $growth$, your incremental volume will be built by key initiative adding y% growth, thus building up to deliver a total plan: x + y = planned growth.

Doing this rigorous planning by key brand, as we look out for the consumer, identify cost reduction opportunities, and keep an eye on accounts receivables, payables, inventory and the competition, affords us superiority in the marketplace and the balance sheet.

It takes tremendous discipline. I manage the company with a behavior model called FACT-A, which I got from one of my predecessors at Tropicana. It stands for Focus, Alignment, Candor, Teamwork, and Accountability. We implement that behavior model across everything we do, ensuring that we have full alignment with our organization. That's not to say we don't have good collegial debate, but once the debate and discussion is over, we move forward as a team, aligned with a single, clear, purpose.

Strategic Planning for Growth and Position

The strategy I use for long-term growth is ultimately based on alternative strategies and growth modeling scenarios I present to the board of directors annually. We only move forward with a strategy once I've gained alignment with the board in terms of how fast we can grow and do so profitably with terrific operating cash flow. Obviously there are many options to pick from, but staying focused on premium brands is the one that will win the day for Galaxy shareholders.

I am positioning Galaxy in the top-performing companies in our industry. Each member of my executive committee understands our mission, vision, and operating values. They know what our specific net revenue, gross margin, and operating and net income needs to be and what is expected in terms of operating cash flow. Thus, each member of my team can make independent decisions with the context of our overall strategy that result in the attainment of our aligned goals.

Then, it's all about the consumer and building a model that delivers superior benefits to the consumer. That model drives our R&D, our quality control, our capital requirements in the plant, and what we need to do in terms of financial management and the partners we pick – from asset-based and capital lenders, all the way through to raising equity on Wall Street. The ability of our organization to secure such resources and partners enables the strategy to come to life; the availability of those resources does not shape the strategy, it's the other way around. Pick the mountain you want to climb, and then set out to secure the resources and tactics needed to successfully climb that mountain. To this end, I am always looking for ways I can grow my premium base brand and then find new avenues for growth among new consumers, new usage occasions, new reasons for consumers to buy, and new benefits.

Measuring Success: More than Numbers

I measure the success of our company and our products on our ability to consistently deliver positive operating cash flow. Our top-line growth, market share, margin, net income, and EBITDA are all secondary to that. Just being a $40 to $50 million net revenue company does not make us successful. Having distribution in 60 percent of all grocery stores does not make us successful. It has to translate into growing operating cash flow. This in turn will make me a successful CEO and enhance shareholder value.

For the company as a whole, the measurement of success goes further than the numbers. While the employees of our company may find these facts something to feel good about, what truly motivates us from a human perspective is that our products benefit people in the universe. Because our products are made from vegetables, with soy, rice, and oats making up our fundamental ingredient component structure, we are doing much to help humanity. And that's a nice benefit that overlays our financial success. While cash flow may be life, doing good for humanity certainly helps to sustain life.

Industry: Desperately Seeking Real Growth

Beyond the standard consolidation of the brokers and the retailers themselves and the manufacturers, I think the industry is changing: It is becoming more desperate to find growth vehicles and avenues for real long-term growth, not just a flash in the pan.

In that desperate approach to the business, I think the industry is starting to take more chances and is becoming less methodical, long term in their thinking and less rigorous about whom they partner with and what SKUs/brands they keep and don't keep on the shelf. So you see multiple competitors with articulation about the same types of benefits but no clear leader or standard as to why they stay or go. As price points widen, that ends up creating a pile of competitors within segments and opens the door for unusual private label growth that will ultimately undermine real sustainable growth in the category. As these and other factors occur, you start seeing a dramatic shift in the ratio of private label to branded products.

Much of this is also driven by speculation about the economy, the high unemployment rate, and pricing pressures, but we at Galaxy compete first and foremost in the premium segment with a premium price and premium quality brand. We find that as long as we continue to deliver with our unique product portfolio against this premise, we still do very well and have high growth rates that create an opportunity for a private label to come in underneath us, but not destroy us. But, there will be no room for duplication among brands and non-discriminate benefits being offered to consumers.

The Future Health of Our Spaceship

I think we will see a huge shift toward belief in the concept that the earth we live on is a spaceship, and it is not an unlimited resource. We may have renewable resources but these must be nurtured and protected. The kinds of products we consume and the way we manufacture and the implications of all that – water, air quality and other natural resources – will become a bigger driver in distinguishing those who make it and those who don't. This transcends brands and pertains to much larger macro trends and eating habits among our society.

The further we move ourselves toward more readily renewable resources – for example, using vegetables versus animal proteins – the more growth we will see in this area that can actually sustain our future population on this earth. Given the population growth rate of our world, there is no way we can sustain ourselves on a meat-based diet. That movement will have a huge impact on the food industry and the beverage industry.

There will always be a need for that kind of food – meats and dairy products. But the ration – how much of that we consume in our diet – will change dramatically. The change won't happen because manufacturers try to make it happen; this change is a world necessity. It's far better to be in front of it than behind it.

Staying Ahead of the Pack

As I mentioned earlier, several Galaxy Foods executives and board members act on and participate in different think tanks, and we are very involved in that respect. We do frequent seminar work where we talk about leading trends. We hold our own out-of-the-box strategic planning sessions, where we gather competitive intelligence and market intelligence and incorporate that into our future thinking.

We also work independently with our vendors, suppliers, and our board members. We have a terrific board of directors at Galaxy Foods who come to us with enormous experience – people previously from Proctor and Gamble, people who ran companies like Dr Pepper/Seven Up and PepsiCo, as well as huge ingredients suppliers, such as Kerry Foods and DCA. We have an individual from a senior position at Cornell University on the board. There is rich, diversified talent at our company that we leverage daily to keep our fingers on the pulse of the trends and add value in our ongoing decisions making.

We also attend and lead activity at some of the largest food tradeshows in the industry. The Produce and Marketing Association is a premier tradeshow that was recently hosted here in Orlando this year. Expo East and Expo West are integral natural food shows. We participate, lead, and try to influence the direction these shows take.

Wish List: A New Playing Field

I continue to push the industry to operate on a fact-based consumer model that forces manufacturers and retailers alike to act on facts and data, along with creation of unique non-duplicable items. I believe doing so would ultimately drive competition to a higher level and enable the people who can do it to market products that are better for the consumer. That seems a far more reasonable proposition than just paying slotting fees to get products on a shelf, only to back a failure that ruins the credibility of both the retailer and the manufacturer.

Using this consumer fact-based model would require some industry standardization on what information is selected and how products are evaluated. It would build a real partnership between the top manufacturers and the retailers, replacing the poker game played now, in which no one shares objectives or valuations or plans for growth. It would result in a whole new playing field of partnerships between manufacturers and retailers on which we would share intelligence and knowledge of each other's business to accomplish our common objectives…attain more consumer dollars.

Bottom-Line Basics for Success: Consumer Marketing, Cash Flow

I expect that the food and beverage industry needs to focus more on the consumer and understand better what the consumers' wants and needs are and what is lacking in the industry regarding those needs. There is no need for "me too" products in this competitive environment.

As that happens, we will see our growth potential unfold explosively. What's happening now in the industry is that it evolves based on what manufacturers throw at consumers. But they aren't helping to monitor the consumer and find out what is really required.

My advice, which I give people in my company and others when I travel, is to be a consumer marketing-driven company, which means understanding consumers and their needs because they're the one thing the entire industry has in common. The consumer happens to buy products at places called retailers and retail outlets, and we, the manufacturers, happen to make products, add value, and ship them to the retailers and retail outlets. If we can meet consumer needs and delight the consumer, then we have a fully aligned end goal.

For everybody, the golden rule is, "Cash flow comes first." You have to have cash flow. You need to build a consumer-driven model that has proprietary benefits and insulation. You need to drive costs out and be efficient so you don't push costs downstream and on to your vendors and your retail partners. And you need to be flexible and open-minded to common goals and how to achieve both of them so there is a win for all partners in the value chain.

Christopher New is currently Chief Executive Officer of Galaxy Nutritional Foods. His responsibilities include planning and directing all aspects of the organization's policies, objectives, and initiatives. He is also responsible for the short- and long-term profitability and growth of the company.

Prior to being elected CEO in December 2002, Mr. New held the position of COO/CMO of Galaxy Nutritional Foods. In this previous assignment, he was in charge of leading, directing, and managing all operational functions including Sales and Marketing activities for the Company.

Before earning a position at Galaxy, Christopher New held the position of Vice President of Commercial Strategies and Services for Tropicana North America and Latin America. He had responsibilities for Strategic Planning, Marketing, Business Development, Sales Planning, E-Commerce, Customer Service, Category Management, and Customer Insights. In his previous assignment he served as Vice President Immediate Consumption Division Marketing, Business Development, North and Latin America. Additionally, Mr. New held the position of Sr. Director of Marketing, New Product and Channel Development and Group Marketing Manager of Chilled and Ambient Season's Best, Beverages and Convenience Store Channel. Before joining Tropicana, Christopher was Sr. Marketing Manager with Motts USA, a division of Cadbury Schweppes.

New is a member of the American Marketers Association. He earned his B.S. at the University of Massachusetts, Amherst in 1982 and his M.S. in Marketing and Economics from Cornell University, Ithaca in 1986.

Changing the Rules for Successful Selling

Peter van Stolk

Founder, President, CEO and Director
Jones Soda Co.

A Changing Industry

Over the last decade or so, there has been huge consolidation in the food and beverage industry, and with that comes greater power and a lot of change. Jones Soda is not adverse to change. We are a young company and that is one of our strengths. We have been doing this since 1996 and we have had to deal with many different ups and downs.

I realized when we started that there was no way we could compete in the food and beverage industry under the existing rules. Those rules were set out by huge companies that have been competing in this category for a long time. With Jones Soda, we had to create a new set of rules and a new way of going to market. Without doing that, I don't think we would be successful. For example, we reach out to customers in a unique way, by allowing them to put their photographs on bottles of our soda. It's fun and it gives them some ownership in the brand.

What Makes a Successful Brand

Products are bought and brands are sought after. The reason people look for brands is that they have formed a connection with them. With products, it's about quality and price. Brands have to work on quality, price *and* image.

You cannot be competitive in today's environment by simply selling a product. There is someone else out there who can make it better, cheaper and faster, thus lowering the price. From my perspective, Jones soda is not a product, but a brand -- otherwise people would be paying a lot less. You can go into a grocery store today and buy 12 cans of private label soda for $1.66 or you can walk into a restaurant and pay $1.75 for one bottle of Jones soda. That is the difference between a product and a brand. I think the most important thing about a brand is that people get excited about it, and in that excitement and enthusiasm, there is a connection.

Our brand has a soul. I know this because I have had hundreds if not thousands of people come up to me and hug me about Jones soda. I have seen tattoos on kids' legs and people parked outside our offices. People send me letters. What I see is that there is an emotional connection between them and this beverage, and that emotion is real. The wonderful thing is that when these big companies do what they call brand retention studies with youth audiences, Jones ranks higher than our size. We don't tell our customers we are cool or that they are cool if they drink Jones soda; Jones simply communicates with our demographic and consumers in a way that creates a connection.

Releasing New Products

Before considering a new product, we look at the enthusiasm within the distributing network. Are the distributors enthused and excited to continue selling your product because they, like anybody, want something new? Then, you look to see what the consumers want. Trends change and tastes change. For example, now everyone is looking to no-carb or low-carb products. You have to be aware of the trends, and you have to be aware of all aspects of the selling environment from the distributor level to the consumer level. That will really dictate when you launch something.

In deciding on a new product, we use a lot of what we feel in our gut because we have been doing this for a long time and we see where we are going. We have what we call influencers, and we ask them questions and we get information from them. They are not researchers or people who sit and look at trends and study focus groups.

If every product were researched and tested in focus groups the way the huge companies do it, there would never be a failure in a product launch because these companies have enough money behind them to make sure people will buy the new product before they launch it. What I don't think they have is the ability to walk the street and really look and see and have vision. The research usually tells you what is already going on, but the vision gives you the time to react to the coming wave.

We have never really advertised or marketed our products other than allowing people to see them in the stores and through what we call in-store marketing. I think one of the things that we have done very, very well is use the web for marketing. We were one of the first beverage companies to have a website, and our site is fun and relevant. It is not just about informing the consumer; it is also about providing information and entertaining them. We will also be marketing with relevant messages using billboard and radio. We focus a lot on packaging as well.

The Challenges of Distribution

The ideal type of distribution is for the products to be consistently in the hands of retailers who want them, and to have distributors who are passionate about the brand. However, the reality is that we work with independent business people who have many different distractions. If

Jones soda were given their full attention, we might sell twice as much beverage as we do currently, but we are only a company of fifty people selling to thirty-eight to forty states. It is hard for us to be everywhere, so we count on other people. Those people sell other things, not just Jones soda.

Currently we work with two distribution channels. One is what we call the independent DSD, or direct store distribution. These are independent distributors who sell a multitude of products. These distributors sell beverages in a community or a territory or region, servicing what is called the independent market. We also deal with some retailers that request us through their own distribution network. Those are really the two primary channels, though we also do a bit of direct consumer sales through our website, where we sell to people who want a case of soda with a certain label on it.

Dealing with the distributors is the most expensive and challenging area that we have to worry about because they have so many choices. Other companies are pulling them in many different directions, and it is just unrealistic for us to think we are going to have their attention every day.

However, we work with only a few retail stores directly through our distributor partners. More often, we sell directly to the retailer using their distributor of choice, which usually is their own distribution network. That is becoming more and more common, and I think that's where the industry is headed.

The retail stores look at three variables when deciding which products to stock. One is profit. Does this make them money and how much profit will they generate from that space in the store? The second is their point of difference. Does this product have a uniqueness that would bring customers to their store vs. another store? Third, does the brand fill a need for that store? In some cases, retailers will put in products that don't meet the first two criteria, but do meet their overall objectives.

The competition is very intense, and it is difficult to take away space from competing products. What we do is to show retailers that Jones soda sells better than our competitors when placed. Retailers want to make money and we believe that our product sells and deserves the space. In addition to sales, we have to show that consumers come to that retailer to find Jones and that Jones creates a positive image for that retailer. If we can hit on all three, that is how we try to get the space.

Goals for the Future

The CEO has to look at the vision and decide where the industry and the company are going. My vision for the food and beverage industry is for small companies to have the opportunity to compete on a level playing field and to provide products that have enthusiasm and energy that this industry has had for the last 100-plus years. If you have multinational corporations running retailers, are consumers going to be given choices or will there just be one company selling to another company? What I would like to see is that consumers are aware of what is going on and appreciate eclectic and unique brands and quality products.

The vision that I have for Jones Soda is to grow it and to create the emotional connection with more and more people. We have to be a company that we are all proud to be a part of and that consumers are proud to be associated with. It is not only about market share, but also about giving something back to the market. Success is obviously monetary, but success for me is also when Jones has done what I think it can do, which is to achieve a certain level of awareness and be recognized as a leader in the beverage industry.

Best Advice

The best piece of advice I could give someone starting their own brand is don't think you have to play by the rules. Others who have far greater resources set the rules in the food and beverage industry. If you do try to play by their rules, you have to remember that you have to have the same amount of resources that they have or you will fail. That is why they were created. For example, slotting fees were originally created to lock out someone else. The rules have to be changed, and new brands can accomplish this by being smarter, faster and more creative, and by looking at things differently. You also need to make sure that people know your brand is real. People are tired of brands that sell them junk. For the small guy who is starting out, that is the key.

Peter van Stolk began in the beverage business when he founded Urban Hand Ltd., a predecessor company to Jones Soda Co., in 1987. Urban Hand Ltd. operated until 1995 as the largest independent distributor of New Age beverages in Western Canada. In 1995, Mr. van Stolk initiated the creation and launch of the Company's own brands, with the launch of its flagship brand, Jones Soda Co. ("Jones Soda" or "Jones"), in 1996. Initially launched into alternative channels of trade with a unique marketing approach including alternative athletes and sampling of Jones Soda via the roving R.V. program, Jones Soda is best known for its innovative labeling technique that incorporates always-changing photos sent in from its consumers. Jones Soda Co. was a pioneer in launching its soda to alternative channels as well as creating an interactive soda, which further allows its consumers to create their own personalized case of "myjones" on-line, becoming the first beverage company to provide value-added and personalized packaging at a price which makes economic sense for both Jones Soda Co. and its consumers. With such a strong emotional connection between the brand and its consumer, Jones has quickly developed a cult-like following in the youth demographic in North America as well as becoming the leader in the premium soda category.

In 2001, Jones Soda Co. extended its product line into the non-carbonated juice and tea category with Jones Juice, utilizing the ever-changing photo concept as well. In this same year, Jones Soda Co. launched Jones Energy, its own energy drink, which has rounded out the Jones brand to include premium soda, juice and teas and an energy drink. The emotional connection between the consumer and the brand is the backbone of Mr. van Stolk's branding strategy and for which he has been recognized by such publications as Advertising Age, Inc. Magazine, The New York Times, CNN, and People Magazine.

Dedication: *To my daughter, Carli.*

Success in the Candy Industry

Herman Goelitz Rowland, Sr.
Chairman of the Board
Jelly Belly Candy Company

A Happy Industry

The candy industry is a happy industry. We make a product that usually puts a smile on someone's face, and just about everyone has a favorite candy. The industry is very broad, appealing to young and old alike. The enjoyment of candy is something everyone has experienced. When people think of candy, they often think of their childhood, but candy isn't only for kids. Adults enjoy a wide range of candy. That's true of what we have seen with many of the candies we make, including Jelly Belly beans.

Candy companies are competitive in a friendly, helpful way. At trade conventions you will find most people are willing to help each other by sharing experiences and using round tables to discuss business issues that we have in common.

At Jelly Belly our goal is to make quality candy for the consumer. We've staked our reputation on quality ever since my great-grandfather started making candy in 1869. Competitor or not, I hate to see lousy candy in the market because it hurts all of us.

Inside the Jelly Belly Candy Company

I started in this business when I was thirteen years old. My parents trained me in every area of the company. I made candy, drove the truck, ordered raw materials and made sales. When you grow up that way, you have a supreme interest in what is happening in all areas of the company. Today, we have six hundred employees, two plants and numerous warehouses.

We are very different from a public company. We do not make decisions to artificially increase our profits, nor do we worry about whether we met our mark this quarter. When we buy equipment or property we know it may affect our margin next year, but it is an investment and profitable in the long run.

To generate growing sales and profits from year to year, we work every day with a passion. We do not leave any stone unturned. We are never satisfied with what we are doing in sales, marketing and production. We always look for the next level of sales, the next marketing opportunity.

What is most important to me is what we are making and what we are selling, rather than our market share. I'm not bothered if we are 5 percent or 20 percent of the total market. What matters to me is whether the product is selling well, if it is working well in the market, and whether we are making a profit.

I consider the company very successful if we have a margin of 10 percent after tax. That is 10 percent after paying a maximum amount to a profit sharing program in which all six hundred employees are enrolled. Our goal is to put the maximum into the program, and if we can do that and make a solid return, then we have achieved our goals.

The most important role I have is to hire incredibly competent and ambitious people who have a desire to contribute and to grow. We are a family company, and we are hiring professional management. We do not hire consultants; we do everything we can from inside. For me the enjoyment of the business is to create your own artwork, develop your own product, build your own buildings and buy your own equipment.

To keep it all on track we have management meetings where we assess what we are doing, and brainstorm the direction we want to take. Our sales and marketing groups meet to review what's happening in the market with our customers. We have a manufacturing group working all the time on how to improve manufacturing. We go to equipment shows to look at new automation product lines. We must continue to automate the company to stay alive. As we grow, we would like to remain with the same number of people because labor is a huge cost of operation. We automate with new technology to accomplish that, which takes a great deal of capital.

Product Development

New products and innovation are supremely important in the candy business. Candy is an impulse purchase for consumers. We need to excite them with new candies, new flavors, new packaging. We constantly work on new Jelly Belly flavors, as well as on entirely new candies. We make candies for all the seasons and candies for every day. We've made chocolate panned candies, jells, candy corn and gummies for years. Many people are surprised to learn we make over a hundred different candies. We recently introduced a new product in the chocolate category called JBz. It has a Jelly Belly flavored shell with a chocolate center and comes in twenty flavors. JBz have been very successful for a candy its first year on the market.

We are always looking at packaging as it relates to different distribution channels. We completely redesigned our packaging this past year to give it a fresh, contemporary look.

The introduction of new flavors of Jelly Belly beans is important to our success. The consumer knows what they are getting when they see Jelly Belly products, and they have high expectations. New flavors add fun and people are interested to try a new taste. We must continue to deliver on that. If we ever fall down on the quality of our product, it would be the end of us.

We hope to introduce a new flavor every year, something the trade asks for at every show we attend. We have fifty official flavors now and a rookie team when new flavors join the lineup. If new flavors are popular, then we rearrange our fifty flavors, so they can join the big league. Last year, we promoted five new rookie flavors.

Because each flavor is so distinct on its own, we recommend people not throw a handful in their mouth, but instead, select the individual flavors they like. We have directions for how to eat our jelly beans, something unheard of before Jelly Belly came along. The experience of each flavor being distinctly different and authentic in flavor is what made Jelly Belly a jelly bean that stood out from the crowd. When we began, jelly beans were a seasonal candy. But the idea that the consumer had the opportunity to select their favorite flavors was novel in 1976.

To introduce a new flavor takes research. First we determine if the taste is recognizable to consumers across the country. Is it a well-known flavor, like banana? Everyone knows what a banana tastes like. How many people know how a kiwi tastes? Not 100 percent to be sure, and kiwi is not a highly distinctive taste. Buttered popcorn has close to 99 percent recognition. Cherry is very recognizable. But a tropical fruit flavor that no one has ever heard of is not going to be successful, even if it has the most wonderful taste imaginable.

Once we determine whether the flavor is well known and recognizable, we will attempt to develop it by using natural ingredients wherever possible. It's not always possible, so we may use combinations of natural and artificial flavors to achieve the authentic taste. We will begin with the actual fruit or food as our standard to match the flavor experience, and we make test batches. Then we eat that candy alongside whatever it is we are trying to reproduce in flavor and aroma. There are some pretty wild flavors we have created that have been widely accepted, because the experience of eating the candy is so surprisingly real. Buttered popcorn is one of those. It was strange to taste a savory flavor in a candy, but it became very popular. It's also a controversial flavor--either you love it or you hate it.

An individual flavor can disappear very quickly. That happens when we misjudged the recognition level by the public believing it was greater than in fact it was. A new flavor may stay in the rookie line for as long as four years to see if it develops a following. The commitment to the variety of fifty flavors makes it a huge effort to change the selection. Every package, mix and menu has to be altered.

We base the success of a new product by how well it is selling. Weekly analysis on all new products on the market helps us keep track. We determine what sold that week and year to date. Every product is reviewed and every seasonal line is reviewed. Since we work more than a year ahead of the season, we must review the season before it is complete in order to determine what we plan to offer the next year.

We work very hard to make the highest quality candy that is also fun to eat. We don't worry so much about the retail price of our candy. We've learned consumers appreciate a quality taste experience, and they know its value.

Importance of Brand Names and Packaging

Brand names are very important. Jelly Belly was created in 1976. David Klein created the idea for the name, but at the time I thought it sounded awful. It did have a catch to it, and the goal was to get people to ask us what a Jelly Belly is so we could tell them. It worked. Today the logo has a 98 percent recognition level among candy consumers. That is just phenomenal. The brand name is so important to our company that a few years ago we changed the name of the company to Jelly Belly Candy Company. It was what everyone called us anyway.

Every bean is printed with the Jelly Belly logo on it. There are other beans out there that imitate us, but they do not have the Jelly Belly logo on the beans. By printing our name on each bean, consumers cannot be deceived when they buy from bulk displays. The idea of printing the name on the beans developed after some stores tried to sell lower priced jelly beans under our name. Early on that was rampant, but we don't see it much anymore.

For a product to sell, consumers need to be attracted to the packaging. The product has to look good. Consistency in color, shape and shine makes our jelly beans stand out from the crowd. At Jelly Belly, we have the candy show through the package so the customer can see the product. We also identify every flavor in the package, usually in pictorial form, so they can pick out the flavors they want, like chocolate pudding, cotton candy, etc. This is an important tool to help them understand that each flavor stands on its own. We also supply "eating directions" that direct consumers to the single flavor experience.

When we started, there were no other products that identified each component in the package. Other manufacturers are trying to catch up to it. We put "recipes" on our packages for combining beans to create a new flavor, like banana split, which requires you to eat six different beans at once. Today, we probably have thirty to forty different recipes. We offer the consumer a level of fun and involvement in our product that no other candy products have.

Advertising, Marketing and Distribution

We came to dominate the jelly bean business because of our consumers, along with some help from President Reagan. We supplied President Reagan with our candy from the time he was governor of California in 1966 until he finished his terms as president, and even to today. In 1981, one of the national news magazines photographed him eating our jelly beans when he was on the presidential campaign. The media wanted to know what he was eating, and the San Jose Mercury News was the first one to mention that our company made his preferred jelly bean. All the media came to our factory. We did not let them in at first because we were scared to death of them. With all the media coverage, orders from our customers poured in. It took us two years to catch up from the ordering frenzy, which put us seventy-seven weeks behind schedule! We were doing incredibly well prior to that exposure, but that breakthrough really stepped up the brand in terms of recognition.

Our company advertises on TV, radio, magazines, newspapers, billboards and bus signs. We have tried sports marketing with racing, golf and bicyclists. We do not have large budgets to work with, so we must be very careful where we spend. For example, we know that women between the ages of eighteen to forty-nine are the largest market for Jelly Belly beans. If you were to look at the demographics of racing, probably 40 percent of the fans are women, which isn't a close enough match. Currently, we are advertising in magazines and radio in specific areas and at cycling events -- 2.5 to 3 million people see those events around the country including quite a few women.

We are also test marketing. We focus on certain areas and create specific advertising in those markets. We are watching sales in the markets to see how much more lift we have. Unfortunately, our budget is not unlimited. I wish we could quadruple the money we spend in this area, but a company has to make a huge margin in order to be able to spend on market tests.

We also opened our factory to the public to come in and see the candy being made. This has been an incredible tool to help consumers understand the efforts we put into making the best candy. We built a Visitor Center to handle all the people, and a half million people came to our California factory last year. They become lifelong fans after taking a tour. It's a huge effort, but it's worth the brand loyalty that comes from the tours. That tour has been so successful that we created a second tour at our distribution center in Wisconsin, which has also been very popular. The tours extend the enjoyment, involve the consumer and get them to taste the candy in a very positive environment.

Thirty years ago, we decided to focus distribution mainly in the "specialty" category, such as gourmet candy stores, gift shops, and department stores. In addition, we sold to distributors and they sold many more accounts. It was a very successful strategy for us, because it allowed us to showcase a large range of single flavor Jelly Belly beans in a prestigious environment. The consumer was attracted by the color and the variety of flavors, which is very engaging. Then the number of candy stores started to decline, because mall locations were so expensive that the stores could not survive. Consumer buying habits changed, too, as new mass market retailers grew into prominence. We wanted to protect the specialty business, but we also needed to expand into the mass market -- grocery stores, drugstores and chains. It broke my heart, but we needed a survival plan.

So we launched a division for that market. Today, the mass market is about half our sales. Consumers are shopping in all types of retail environments and they bring their desire for quality candy with them, which the large chains have responded to by expanding candy and bringing in better quality candy.

Candy is generally a high impulse purchase, so in-store placement is very important as a sales tool. It is essential for candy to have exposure near the traffic areas in the stores because that drives sales. Checkout counters are a great impulse area. As an industry we fight for space.

Market Price and Competition

The stores determine market price. Stores have particular margins that they seek. That usually determines within a few dollars a pound what the price is going to be. I see Jelly Belly selling in the market between $6.00 and $8.00 a pound depending on the store, and whether they are selling straight or assorted flavors. I am starting to see $10.00 a pound for bulk Jelly Belly. The reason is the cost of operations. In these big malls, the square footage price is so high they have to get more money per pound for the product. Those issues drive what the price is going to be.

To take away shelf space from a competing product, we demonstrate how well our candy sells. We show specific figures, product margins and profit per linear foot of shelf space for our items versus other products. In the gourmet business retailers know us and count on us as a major supplier of top selling candy. They also buy from us because we have committed our company to providing superior customer service. We make shipments complete and on time, and if there is a problem, we take care of it immediately. The company gains a reliable reputation that way. It is important to us not only to have quality candy but also to have quality service. People get used to that, recognize it and appreciate it.

Challenges and Frustrations of the Candy Business

The federal and state regulations are the largest frustrations in this business. Every day there seems to be more laws and more new regulations to follow. This makes me livid. Right now, there is paperwork on my desk waiting for my signature. I will read every word before I sign.

The greatest difficulties we have are with state and federal regulations on health and welfare. This year, medical costs and workers compensation are going to cut our margins by two thirds. We are scrambling to deal with that. You can only increase the price of your product so much, and we cannot raise it enough to offset those costs. The challenge is how to stay in business with these increasing costs.

Also, inheritance tax affects a small business like ours. I am the fourth generation in this company and I have four children and a son-in-law in the business. I want them to have the company, but it is going to be a terrible struggle, even though I planned for the last fifteen years for it. The harder I work and the better the company does, the harder it will be for my kids to own the company after my death. We pay taxes on everything now and when I die, 50 percent of it will get taxed again. The exemptions go up to something like $2 million, but when you have property and land and equipment, it's not enough.

I feel there is a glimmer of hope. I have great confidence in our new California governor Arnold Schwarzenegger. He is the first breath of fresh air since Reagan. One of his pledges is to lift the regulations off the back of California businesses, so businesses have the ability to stay here and new businesses have the interest to come here.

In addition, in the past five to ten years the increased regulations on labeling have been a challenge. I believe it is important to have the information there, but they change it so frequently, and then all the packaging in the country has to be changed. It is an enormous expense and a huge waste.

Future Trends and Changes in the Candy Industry

The candy industry will continue to change, year after year, decade after decade. We see huge issues come up, such as GMOs, which are genetically modified products, such as where corn is altered to be resistant to insects. Half the food in the world probably comes from GMO products. And so when people claim GMO is poison, it is a problem. We lost a huge account in the U.K. because of it.

The corn that is grown in America is either GMO corn or it is grown in a field next to GMO corn. There is no way to buy corn syrup in this country that is certified GMO free. But when it goes through the process of being made into corn syrup, no GMO proteins remain. We have our candy analyzed and it is GMO free. The debate has quieted down a bit, but some regions are still struggling with it.

I think candy always comes back again. From the consumers' point of view, candy is a fun way to give themselves a treat without spending a huge amount of money. During recessions and hard times, the candy business usually does well because of that fact. When times are good, candy still sells well. What bothers me is seeing candy in the market that is poor quality. I think it reflects badly on all candy makers to have this low-quality candy in the market. Most of it is coming from Mexico, Canada and South America. Many of these companies left the U.S. because of the cost of sugar here. It costs us $0.30 a pound here, but only $0.13 a pound over the border. That's because the U.S. subsidizes the farmers. We are stuck paying these high rates for sugar and we cannot compete with the rest of the world.

Many candy companies have left because of that and the cost of labor. Mexican labor costs $13 a day and labor in China is $75 a month. We're a family company that wants to make candy in America with American labor and it is our goal today to stay that way.

Herman G. Rowland is chairman of the board of Jelly Belly Candy Company headquartered in Fairfield, Calif. The firm manufactures Jelly Belly® jelly beans and 100 Confections® by Jelly Belly gourmet candies.

Rowland went to work for his parents at the age of thirteen in the Oakland, Calif. plant, of the then Herman Goelitz Candy Co., the firm his grandfather established on the west coast. In 1959 Rowland went into the business full time. As a confectionery apprentice he learned the skills of candy making from the ground up. Throughout the 1960s and early 70s, Rowland expanded his knowledge and expertise and, when the firm incorporated in 1975, he was named president.

In 1976 Rowland accepted a challenge from a California entrepreneur to develop a jelly bean made with "natural" ingredients for flavorings. The intensely flavored Jelly Belly jelly bean was created using real fruit purees and other natural ingredients whenever possible and became an immediate success. In the years since, Rowland has been an innovator for many "firsts" in candy making, such as the nine-inch long Pet Rat®, Prehistoric Eggs and the biggest gummi candy ever brought to market, a two-and-a-half-foot gummi snake.

He was honored for lifetime achievement in 1988 and awarded the prestigious Kettle Award. Rowland was also inducted into the Candy Hall of Fame in 1989 by the National Confectionery Sales Association of America and honored with the Henry J. Bornhofft Memorial Award from the Retail Confectioners International trade organization in 1987.

In 1978, Rowland's company acquired a majority interest in the original family firm, Goelitz Confectionery Company in North Chicago, where his grandfather started in the business. Rowland's cousin, William Kelley, was president of that operation until the two companies merged under the Jelly Belly Candy Co. name in April 2001. Kelley is now vice chairman of the board.

Brewing for Quality

Jim Koch

Founder and Brewer
The Boston Beer Company
(Brewer of Samuel Adams)

Brewing Beer

Brewing is an art that began 6,000 years ago and it incorporates centuries of tradition. On the other hand, there is a lot of science involved in brewing. Brewing brings together years of art and science.

At Samuel Adams, we compete against large domestic and international brewers that are often parts of huge conglomerates. We bring a genuine passion for beer and appreciation for the brewer's craft. I am actually the sixth oldest son to be a brewer in my family. I got a recipe from my dad and brewed it in my kitchen to start with, and then brewed it at a pilot lab at the Fermentation Sciences School in California. Eventually, I made a test batch at a full-scale brewery.

Getting Started in the Beer Business

When I started Sam Adams, I set out to change the way Americans think about domestic beer. My initial strategy was simply to make better beers and then to enter them in brewing contests and beer festivals. I had faith that if the beers were truly better, they would win awards and that would validate the idea that Sam Adams beers really are better than beers from well-known international brewers.

My mission was to get drinkers to believe that an American brewer really was brewing world-class beer. I built the business bar by bar and drinker by drinker. To get our products into bars, I just put cold beer in my briefcase and went from bar to bar getting bartenders and bar owners to sample my beer. Most of them liked it and ordered it. Once it hit the bars, drinkers began to discover the quality of our beers and they were open to the new beer that we offered. Our commitment to use only the best ingredients and best recipes, plus the care and passion we infused into the brewing process, brought drinkers to us.

Brewing the Best Beer

In order to develop a successful product that will be around for years, you have to have a single-minded devotion to the quality of the product and resist the temptation to change it based on trends and fashions. If you have something really wonderful, people will find it and keep buying your product.

We will change the packaging every so often, but we are not trying to be the latest and greatest. We are just trying to be the best. We charge more money for our beer so we have to give the consumer a reason to spend more. The ingredients are more expensive and we use them in larger quantities. The beer takes longer to make and there is a lot more care and attention that goes into every batch. I go as far as sampling every batch of Samuel Adams myself to be sure that we uphold our commitment to quality.

When we decide on pricing for our product, we figure out how much it is going to cost to make a truly great beer and that determines the price. Our most expensive beer is called Samuel Adams Utopias. It is 50 proof, making it the strongest beer in the world, and it sells for $100 a bottle.

Packaging is not that important–success is mostly a result of the quality and taste of the beer. We chose a standard beer bottle when packaging. It was important for us to put the beer in a brown bottle because that is the only way to protect it from light, which makes beer skunky. We make sure our beer is always fresh by putting consumer-friendly dating on the beer. If we find beer that has passed its freshness date, we pull it from the shelves.

Releasing a New Product

The research that goes into developing a new product is basically a lot of drinking. We drink different brews and test them against other beers. It's all tasting and drinking beer. For example, I just finished a tasting of four different brews of a new beer that we are thinking of releasing. Once we have the best version of that style available to American beer drinkers, we release it. We won't release something unless we believe that it is the best in America of that style.

We want to be the best and most innovative brewer in the world. We want to make more award-winning beers than any other brewer. To do that, a product needs to have quality and unique character. It has to be good and it can't be a "me too." It has to be different.

Advertising and Marketing Strategies

Our best advertising is by word of mouth. We do a lot of waitstaff training at retailers where one of our salespeople will come in and bring malt and hops. They talk about the brewing process and how our beer is made and then let them taste different beers so they can see the difference between really good hops and mediocre hops. We will often have them taste Sam Adams and then some other beers so they can taste the difference.

Distribution

Our biggest distribution channels are bars and restaurants. After that, it is grocery stores, then independent liquor stores, depending on the state. The bars, restaurants and stores are looking for something that will sell and also something that is high quality. They determine quality by drinking the beer and by its reputation.

In our business, it is very important to work with distributors because the distributor is the one who actually reaches the retailer. We are not allowed to sell to retailers because of the three-tier system. Every state regulates alcohol slightly differently. One consistent thread is a brewer sells to a wholesaler and then the wholesaler sells to the retailer and the retailer sells to the consumer. That is the law. In order to export beer overseas, we have to have a distributor that we think can maintain our quality standards. Every country has its own unique laws about importing beer.

Growing Revenues and Profits

In order to continue generating revenues and profits from year to year, we need to make interesting beers and maintain our standards of quality. We have to continue to interest and excite the beer drinker. We currently have about fifteen styles of beer. Some we make once a year. We are working now with Scharffen Berger, a chocolate maker on the west coast, to develop a new brew, Samuel Adams Chocolate Bock.

The most costly parts are the ingredients and the cost of operating the brewery. Samuel Adams takes two or three times as long to brew as many other beers because we age it longer to get a smoother beer. That means that we need more aging tanks to make Sam Adams beer, so it is a bigger investment.

Most Challenging Parts of the Business

The most challenging part of the business is continuing to educate American beer drinkers about the quality of their own beer. We do staff tastings and I have done radio ads for eighteen years to talk about the brewing process, the ingredients and the different styles of beer we make. We have a brewery in Boston and tens of thousands of people visit every year to learn about Samuel Adams.

Another challenge in the industry is that we are always the little guy. We don't produce beer for the mass market so we are always going to be about quality and not quantity. We are not trying to mass-produce enormous quantities of beer, we are just trying to make world-class American beer every day.

As a CEO, I worry about the quality of the beer and the quality of the people that work for me. I look for people who are passionate about what we do and who are committed to developing their own skills and who are open and honest. I also look at how to position the company to thrive on change in the marketplace. We try to drive it by leading people and showing them new beers, changing ideas about what beer can be and creating a sense of adventure around quality brewing.

Measuring Success

We measure success of the company and products by the awards that we win and by the evaluations we get from our wholesalers and our own people as well as whether we are maintaining our passion for beer. When we started, we were picked as "The Best Beer in America" for four years running. That put us on the map. The company was two people when we won it the first year.

Sam Adams has been successful in educating Americans about different styles of flavorful beer. Today, people are not surprised to walk into a bar and see a range of good beers such as an amber lager or seasonal beers. People are now turned on to variety and quality in American beer. When I started, quality American beer was an oxymoron.

Globally, we have become known as a very unique brewer bringing back classic brewing traditions in a market that many saw as all about watered-down, mass-produced beer. Brewers in Germany, England and Australia are becoming aware of Sam Adams as one of the great brewers of the world. Last week we had the Association of Small and Independent German Breweries at our brewery to try to understand what we were doing and how we are successful.

Customer service is also an area where we measure success. Our customers are not only beer drinkers but also the retailers and the wholesalers, so customer service is crucial. Because beer has a limited freshness life, if a distributor has too much inventory on a product, we may move it all the way across the country. We have one hundred and eighty salespeople all over the country that work strictly for Sam Adams.

Best Advice

The best piece of advice for someone who is just starting out in the beverage industry would be to start small and make sure you have a very high quality product that is unique and different. You need to have faith in the quality of what you are doing and start small and work hard.

When I first started out, a case of Heineken cost $14 and a case of Sam Adams cost $20. I was small and I did not have any economy of scale, so that is what I needed to charge. I wasn't bashful about the price, because I knew it was better to charge more so that I wouldn't have to compromise on the quality of the ingredients or the brewing process.

Jim Koch sparked a nationwide revolution in quality American brewing by producing beers that Americans haven't tasted for a hundred years, and has won more international awards for brewing than any brewer in the world.

Koch was born into an American family originally from Germany with deep roots in brewing beer -- first in Germany then St. Louis during the Civil War. While he was growing up, a few huge multinational companies controlled America's supply of beer. Small local breweries were closing all over the country. Koch's father retired from the beer business and he went on to Harvard for a "liberating" education.

At Harvard, Koch took overlapping course loads for advanced degrees in both business and law. As a management consultant, Koch counseled the leaders of client corporations at the Boston Consulting Group. For six years, CEOs learned from Koch, and he learned from them. Koch decided to start a business of his own – to become a brewer in the fashion of five generations of Kochs before him. Koch turned to his father for advice, and got both advice and his first investor out of the conversation. He also got the cornerstone of The Boston Beer Company: the long-abandoned recipe from his great great-grandfather for making the "better beer" that his family had brewed when Ulysses S. Grant was telling war stories in the White House.

He made the first batch of beer in his kitchen according to the old ways. He insisted then, as now, that only the world's best ingredients will make the best beer, and that quality and flavor were the only standards worth pursuing. He wanted a world-class beer for America, and he made one in 1984. With a few bottles of really good beer, Koch made brewing a person-to-person business. When local distributors declined to carry the brew, he carried chilled bottles of his beer to bartenders around Boston. They thought Koch was doing the right thing by brewing small batches of beer with a focus on flavor and an obsessive eye on quality. They also thought naming the beer after Samuel Adams, a patriot who had led the colonies into the American Revolution, made sense.

Koch built the business outward from his first accounts in Boston. Six weeks after the introduction, Samuel Adams was picked as "The Best Beer in America" at The Great American Beer Festival. The Company has since won more international brewing medals than any other brewery in the world.

The success of Sam Adams Boston Lager is credited with leading the renaissance in American taste for fresh, better beers. The success is also credited with the explosion of brewpubs and microbreweries in America, and later the "craft brewing" movement.

Management Best Sellers

Other Best Sellers

- Ninety-Six and Too Busy to Die - Life Beyond the Age of Dying - $24.95

- Technology Blueprints - Strategies for Optimizing and Aligning Technology Strategy and Business - $69.95

- The CEO's Guide to Information Availability - Why Keeping People and Information Connected is Every Leader's New Priority - $27.95

- Being There Without Going There - Managing Teams Across Time Zones, Locations and Corporate Boundaries - $24.95

- Profitable Customer Relationships - CEOs from Leading Software Companies on using Technology to Maxmize Acquisition, Retention and Loyalty - $27.95

- The Entrepreneurial Problem Solver - Leading CEOs on How to Think Like an Entrepreneur and Solve Any Problem for Your Team/Company - $27.95

- The Philanthropic Executive - Establishing a Charitable Plan for Individuals and Businesses - $27.95

- The Golf Course Locator for Business Professionals - Organized by Closest to Largest 500 Companies, Cities and Airports - $12.95

- Living Longer Working Stronger - 7 Steps to Capitalizing on Better Health - $14.95

- Business Travel Bible - Must Have Phone Numbers, Business Resources, Maps and Emergency Info - $19.95

- ExecRecs - Executive Recommendations for the Best Business Products and Services Professionals Use to Excel - $14.95

Call 1-866-Aspatore or Visit www.Aspatore.com to Order